SALLY MORGAN'S

My Place

A CRITICAL STUDY

SALLY MORGAN'S

My Place

A CRITICAL STUDY

Edited by

Reena Mitra

R K Dhawan

Prestige

an international publishing house

Published by
Prestige Books
3/28, East Patel Nagar
New Delhi 110 008
Ph. 9818755529
email: prestigebooks@gmail.com
website: asiabookclub.com

Associate Office
60/29-45 Parramatta Road,
Concord, NSW 2137
Australia

ISBN: 81-7851-051-0

Printed at Chaman Offset Press, New Delhi 110 002

Contents

Critical Perspectives

Introduction

Sally Morgan, born in the city of Perth in Western Australia in 1951, studied Psychology at the University of Western Australia and acquired a degree and various post-graduate diplomas in Counselling Psychology, Computers and Library Studies from the Western Australian Institute of Technology. Her major published works are *My Place, Wanamurraganya, The Story of Jack McPhee*, a children's text titled *Dan's Grandpa* and a play, *Sistergirl*. What is most relevant here is that in conformity with the spirit of her works, the Human Rights and Equal Opportunity Commission's 1987 award for Literature was bestowed upon her. Also, in 1989, she was awarded the Western Australian citizen of the year award for Arts, Literature and Culture.

Besides being a writer of potential, Sally Morgan has also given evidence of her genius as a visual artist and has works exhibited in the Australian National Gallery, Canberra and the Dobell Foundation Collection. Her paintings communicate ideas and themes similar to those expressed in *My Place*, for instance, the primacy of land, the importance of birds and snakes in human existence and the significance of spirit life and political ideas as represented in *Terra Nullius*. Morgan's visual acuity is reflected in the quotidian activities of her characters that she records in her writings.

The importance and relevance of a text does not depend on its form but on the correlation between that text and its audience or readership. *My Place* has been a consequential text because the readers are cognizant of the historical importance of Morgan's story and relate effortlessly to her character and disposition. Fictionalised versions of lives and circumstantial facts as we witness in this particular work, *My Place*, become rather significant if they are able to change the outlook and perspective of their readers in some way or the other.

Both biography and autobiography are both literary genres that often interest and fascinate readers because they represent the individual aspect of the experience of the community as a whole. These texts, if they illuminate historical issues and put them in the right perspective, become significant. They project the spirit of the times and depict the historical milieu of the period in a convincing manner. *The Letters of Rachel Henning*, written over a span of almost thirty years, that is, between 1853 to 1882, have been collected to be presented in an autobiographical form. They are approached today not only as an assessment of Henning's personal life but also as an understanding and consciousness of Australian history.

My Place has made a mark in Australian literature because of the tremendous impact it has had on young minds, changing their entire attitude to their Aboriginal derivation and heritage. In it, the bulk of the text is written in the first person singular and simulates an autobiography. The reader learns much about Sally and her family through her digressive and episodic style of writing. He/she is insidiously drawn into Sally's quest for her lost identity and cannot but empathize with her in her attitude to her past. The biographical events referred to in the story support Sally's statements and assertions and lead the reader to be outraged by past discrimination and injustices. The reader now appreciates Daisy's expressed desire for privacy as well as Arthur's openness in sharing his story with others. My place would have lost its appeal and its sense of secrecy and revelation if it had been completely fictionalized. The blend of biography and autobiography offered has proved to be the most convincing way of making one believe in the historical integrity of the narrative and in Sally's change of perspective.

In order to depict the Australian society of a particular period from a specific point of view, both *The Dish* and *Looking for Alibrandi* present fictionalized biography. Like *My Place*, they aim at moulding people's attitudes and changing the course of their actions for the better. The successes of these works have shown that fiction can rival the literary forms of biography and autobiography in terms of the impact it can forge.

Looking for Alibrandi is a fictionalized form of Melina Marchetta's life that includes inputs from other members of her community. The Australian readers have been significantly influenced by the text and its historical and emotional intensity. Marchetta has shown in her work the notable personal change that is perceived in a young Australian girl with an Italian background. There is a film version of this too. The other work referred to, *The Dish*, offers an imaginary version of the role of the Parkes Tracking station in relaying the pictures from Apollo 11 in 1969. The film presents biographical snippets of three men working at the station and their NASA co-worker. Also depicted is a general view of the townspeople at the time. The historical version has been cleverly fictionalized and personal change is seen in all the men and more so in the leader, all of whom learn through their experience of the moon landing. The portrayal of the society of the times is recognizably convincing and authentic.

However, though there have been other texts like *My Place*, the latter has certainly had an unprecedented impact and a great influence on the Australians, whose search for lost identity has required patience and resolution in bringing about desired personal changes in the people of the country. This work, Sally Morgan's first published composition, was written over a stretch of about nine years spanning the period from 1979 to 1987. She needed to elicit hitherto concealed information from the members of her family to be able to complete the text and once this was done verification of records and travel to Port Hedland and Marble Bar for more insights followed.

Originally since *My Place* was written as a genealogical survey of the author's family, she intended to have only ten copies of the text printed. She avoided including in the narrative elaborate discussions of the more general and comprehensive issues affecting Aboriginal people such as questions of land rights, reconciliation and deaths in custody. The renown and distinction attained by her book, however, brought her into the public view and people started expecting her to be a spokesperson of these various above mentioned matters in question. Her writings, however, as said before, were never intended to be public and political. Her target was the bulk of ordinary Australians to whose notice she brought these issues in a non-conflictual manner.

The title of the work, *My Place*, is a colloquial term with a multiplicity of meanings. "My Place" can refer to the physical location of a person in his house or to his position at a dinner table. The word "place" can refer to one's social position or have a spiritual connotation as observed in the expression "one's place in the scheme of things." What needs to be understood here is that in the Aboriginal culture, physical place and spiritual place are correlated. *My Place* is an odyssey of discovery and revelation incorporating all these concepts of "place." It is an excursion into and an exploration of life leading to a celebration of self-actualization and self-understanding. It is a journey that brings consciousness and growth, a journey that takes the protagonist from one point of understanding to another. Essentially *My Place* is a search for identity that takes Sally from ignorance to knowledge.

The title of *My Place*, significant as it is, is markedly ironic because in the past years, Daisy and Gladys Corunna had managed to establish and retain "their place" in Australian society by concealing the factuality of their Aboriginal origins and ancestry. Their parentage and race had to be kept in wraps for them to be able to live.

Sally Morgan's *My Place*, first published in 1987, was prompted by her discovery of her Aboriginal descent and is largely autobiographical in tone and spirit. It refers to her marriage to Paul Morgan whom she had met while doing her courses at the University and describes her family life in which her husband and her three children figure prominently. The focus in the work, however, is on the life of the Corunna family and the text incorporates the narratives of Sally's Uncle Arthur, her Nan, Daisy, and her mother, Gladys. It is through these tales that the text is structured and the reader knows as little as Sally does. The latter's quest for truth regarding her past is closely followed by the reader, too, but there is no formal resolution of problems as in the unravelling of an initially inscrutable and impenetrable mystery. With stoic fortitude and equanimity, Morgan unearthed her Aboriginal tribe and skin groups, her land and relatives, all she had been ignorant about earlier. With her growing closeness to her grandmother came the burgeoning consciousness and cognizance of her roots. It is this awareness of her Aboriginal, familial, spiritual and personal identity that inspired her to proclaim her ancestry with a sense of pride and self-esteem.

Sally Morgan's was a focused attempt at exploring and establishing the truth regarding her progenitors and tracing her genealogy as far back as possible. Had she diverted into a description of the political situation at Yandcarra, she would have foiled her purpose of recounting her family history. It was only Sally's persistent effort that made her grandmother, Daisy, begin telling her story, but only when she was terminally ill and was animated into narration by the stories from other areas read out to her by her grandchildren. Gladys, Daisy's daughter, was removed from the family before she was old enough to register such stories and thus, Sally in turn, was never told any.

All literary artists, in recording in words what they wish to, fall back upon past works either to conform to or differ from the established tradition and thus, the pastness of the past becomes a very significant factor in any new composition. Morgan had a tradition of Aboriginal work to refer to like the works of Kevin Gilbert, Colin Johnson, Jack Davis etc. She also had an accessible tradition of biography and autobiography as illustrated in *The Diary of Anne Frank*. It is from a combination of all these text types that she created a different genre of work. In this context, one may refer to *Silent Legacy* as using the same method of reconstructing the past as Morgan but the essential difference of medium remains, for *Silent Legacy* is a film and not a written text.

An important aspect of the text of *My Place* is its setting in Australia. Placing the narrative in its historical context, the text explores the inhuman treatment meted out to the native people of Australia, the Aborigines. The Aboriginal tribes in the country formed a society in which they needed to define their kinship structures so that social interaction between tribal groups could be facilitated. Relationships within a group were streamlined through the framing of rules governing them. Each individual, initiated into his/her tribe at puberty knew his/her group and the totem associated with it. The rituals associated with initiation often included body-scarring as corroboration of the accomplishment of initiation. Also, each tribe had men with magic powers and the Aboriginals looked upon them with awe. In *My Place*, the term used for a man endowed with the competence to perform magic is called a *boolyah man*.

After establishing a Federation in 1901, all the states of Australia developed and implemented their own specific Acts for the protection of Aboriginal people. The Protection Acts of the various states had certain common features like the following:

1) Aboriginal people did not have the right to vote.
2) The Aboriginals could leave their reserves for a very short time and only with the permission of the Manager. Besides, each had to carry a permit.
3) The children of the Aborigines were wards of the State and could be separated from their parents and placed in Homes. Daisy briefly describes the life of her cousin, Helen Bunda, at the Moori River reserve. In *My Place,* Gladys was placed in the Parkerville Children's Home which was under the Church administration and was referred to as a mission. Arthur, Sally's uncle, was taken to the Anglican Mission on the Swan River in Fremantle. These homes separated children with lighter skins from those with darker skins, and often, the former were adopted by the Whites.
4) In Western Australia, no Aboriginal could be paid a wage without the approval of the Government.
5) Aboriginal people could be arrested without a warrant, and
6) It was illegal for a White person to marry an Aboriginal without the Protector's permission. Under the provisions of the *Aborigines Act* of 1905, the Whites were not even allowed to socialize with the Aboriginals or have relationships with them.

All the tribal children were given a basic education and were trained in domestic chores so that when they became fourteen, they could be sent to work for White families but without any remuneration. However, the worst experience was the trauma and pain of being separated from their parents and tribe, often for good, and the subsequent sense of deprivation regarding the acquisition of knowledge of themselves or their culture.

As for the language of the Aborigines, there was no single language used all over the country. In *My Place* Arthur communicates that the people at Corunna Downs spoke *Balgoo* and *Naml* which were both dialects of the same language and Arthur himself spoke also *Nungamurda* and *Nybali.* A number of Aboriginal languages have become defunct and are no longer used because of the Government policy of forbidding the use of Aboriginal languages and compelling the children of the various tribes to learn English.

At the beginning of World War I, Aboriginal men were not permitted to enlist in the Army but after the massacres of 1915 the government rules were relaxed and they were allowed to fight for Australia. However, with the 1967 referendum giving control of Aboriginal affairs to the Commonwealth Government, there has been a consciousness of the need for reconciliation between the Aboriginals and the Whites.

Plot

My Place is framed as an excursion leading to the discovery of Sally Morgan's Aboriginal descent. She recounts in chronological order the sequence of events that led her to the discovery of her tribal past and thereby enables the reader to share her past experiences, to realize the enormousness of the difficulties she had to encounter and to gauge the satisfaction she lived through in recording the narratives of her relatives. The importance and significance Morgan gives to the separate stories of Arthur, Gladys and Daisy shows the respect she has for them. The structural framework of the plot reveals that the voyage of discovery is made not only by Sally but by all the members of her family and hence, the text can claim the status not of an autobiography but of a chronicle of events in the history of a family.

My Place is structured as a concatenation of the four autobiographies of Sally Morgan, Arthur Corunna, Gladys Corunna and Daisy Corunna, all of which are linked by Sally's pursuit of the truth about her family history and by her need to assert her own Aboriginal identity. These four life-stories are concurrent at certain critical periods in the lives of the authors and it is because of this overlapping that it is possible to confirm the facts that each reports and to see the events and characters from different perspectives. Sally, for example, refers to Frank Potter as a saviour of the family after Dad died. She realizes that Gladys did not really care for him because he drank but she welcomed his gifts of food that came regularly. In Gladys's story we are told that Frank's reappearance in the life of Bill Milroy had revived his nightmares and hastened his collapse. It is, however, the two stories together that enable the reader to size up the character of Frank more accurately.

The various stories in the text are interwoven in more ways than one. Arthur's story inspired Sally to go to Corunna Downs and thus, his narrative determined the direction of the next part of the latter's account. Also, Daisy's story narrated on her death-bed enabled Sally to clinch the text with an affirmation of Daisy's life and her own Aboriginal descent.

Totems were part of the process by which Sally learned to internalize the experience of being an Aboriginal and as such are significantly central to her sense of belonging and identity. All through the text of *My Place* there are references to birds and animals in connection with different characters. Daisy was closely connected with birds. When young she spent her time observing magpies as well as catching cockatoos and setting them free. She educated the children in all kinds of wildlife for this was very important to her. Her death, too, was associated with the bird call, which had for her a spiritual significance.

Gladys, on the other hand, related to wildlife only indirectly, mainly through programmes on the television. Since she had been given an initiation scar by Daisy at birth, Gladys must have had a totem but she never discussed this. Sally, however, learned about the Rainbow Serpent and snakes and, conscious of their centrality, represented them in her paintings. Besides, there are regular references to swans in connection with Perth for the black swan is the formal emblem for Western Australia.

Daisy Corunna was born around the year 1900, that is, before the protection law was passed in Western Australia but it came to be implemented by the time she was old enough to be removed and thus, only Arthur, Albert and Katie were removed from Corunna Downs. Alice Drake-Brockman apparently violated the law several times. She herself admitted that she had been prosecuted for taking Daisy to Perth but won the case. As for Gladys, although she did not keep her when she was at Parkerville, she broke the law again in obtaining the florist's apprenticeship for her.

Another important aspect of the plot is the fact that Daisy never told her family that she could speak two Aboriginal languages because she did not want them to know about their Aboriginal heritage. As Aboriginal languages were taboo in schools, the use of any Aboriginal word would have identified the Aboriginal affiliations of the children and hence they were kept away from all languages of this community.

My Place is an intensive and compact text offering graphic descriptions and factual details in the course of the main narrative. A summary of the work, however, cannot reproduce the tone and spirit of the text. Neither can it depict the emotional impact of the composition on the reader yet, a plot summary is a vital and useful study guide for academic purposes.

My Place: A Textual Analysis

Chapter One: The Hospital

Sally Morgan's narrative begins with the details of her visits to the hospital where her father was admitted because of his mental ailments. Her visits were of importance not only to her father but also to the other soldiers in the hospital. She defines her relationship with her grandmother, Nan, who is known as Daisy Corunna and who lives in the Milroy family house. When she was a child, Nan sometimes woke her up early and took her outside to observe wildlife. These experiences were fascinating and magical whereas her trips to the hospital made her sad. This chapter also describes briefly the complex relationship between her Mum and Dad caused by the latter's problems. It concludes with the birth of Sally's brother, David, in 1957, and foreshadows the future events.

Chapter Two: The Factory

Sally's early experiences at school when she was six were not very happy ones. The teacher, Miss Glazberg, took custody of the children and asked the mothers to leave. Sally learned to read quickly but developed a dislike for school. Out of sheer perversity, when given good art paper to draw a picture for the parent teacher night, she drew her parents naked. Now when Sally comes home from school, she is allowed certain privileges like staying up late with her father who is in and out of hospital because of his wartime trauma and is consequently, often without work. Mum works as a part-time cleaner to support the family. Dad is inclined to turn violent and one night he pushes Mum over.

Chapter Three: I'm in the Army Now

Jill, Sally's sister, joins her at school and is surprisingly confident and cool. Sally's new teacher, Miss Roberts, has been in the Women's Army and is very masculine in appearance and manners. Sally wets her pants in her class and feels humiliated at being turned out of the class room.

Chapter Four: Drinking Men

Dad's condition worsens and Sally's home-life seems to be falling apart because of her father's continual drinking, which is largely responsible for the family's poverty. All Sally's father's friends and uncles drink except Uncle John.

At Christmas the house is cleaned, cakes and puddings are made and Nan kills a chook for dinner. The Milroys come out for dinner and Grandpa talks about the members of his family being gamblers and drinkers. Sally shows interest in drinking and smoking, but hates the taste of beer.

Dad had bought a 1948 Ford van in which he takes the family for a picnic to Roleystone. The children collect stones, insects, wildflowers etc. for Nan. Dad terrifies everyone by the way he reverses the van.

Chapter Five: Pretending

Billy, Sally's brother, starts school in 1959 but he does not quite like it and often pretends to be sick to take the day off from his studies in school. Sally imitates him in trying to look pale and sick by powdering her face. Mum has a part time job in Boans' Floral Department. Sally and Jill are together in Grades Two and Three which are a composite class.

Sally begins to observe the socio-economic differences between groups at school. Her sister, Helen, is born in April and Sally is told that babies grow under cabbages.

Sally comes to realize that other children do not relate to their families as well as she and her siblings do. Mum and Nan try to hide their Aboriginal origin and instruct the girls to tell everyone that they are Indian.

Chapter Six: Only a Dream

When Sally is about eight, her Dad's hospital visits become more and more frequent for his inclination towards violence increases. The family often has to take refuge in Aunty Grace's house behind their own when Dad is in a violent mood for even Sally, towards whom he is never aggressive, fails to appease him at such times.

Chapter Seven: A Change

Sally does plenty of reading and drawing in the second term of her fourth year for she likes both the activities. Before getting to paint with oil colours which were given to her by someone, she draws in the sand, and elsewhere, with charcoal.

By this time, the family resources are drained out since Dad's intake of beer has increased manifold. To satiate his urge for drinking, he takes money even from the children's money box. To make things worse, he rents a television and this is another hole in the pocket. Arthur, Nan's brother, visits the family at this time with his children. Sally thought they were Indian. Arthur Corunna becomes a key character in her exploration later.

Dad comes home from the hospital for Jill's birthday and sits drinking on the verandah to provoke Mum. In November, he asked for Billy to be left alone with him and that is when he dies. The other children, when they come, see Dad carried away in an ambulance and Mrs. Mainwaring, a neighbour, tells them that he is dead.

Chapter Eight: Family and Friends

Sally is afraid that the children would now be put in an orphanage. But, instead, Billy, at the age of six, is made the man of the house and he takes his new responsibility very seriously. The Coroner's report said that Dad had committed suicide due to a war-induced condition, so Mum is granted a war pension. A neighbour is romantically inclined towards Mum but the latter promises the children that she will not remarry. She gets her driving licence and they all visit the Milroy grandparents.

The children's lives are changed for the better and Gladys, Sally's mother, becomes far more independent now. She has to take many part-time jobs to support her five children. The family is still struggling with finances but family, friends and their Legatee, Mr. Willie, help them in times of need.

Chapter Nine: Wild Life

The Milroy house is full of pets. They had thirteen cats but have now given half away. When one dog dies, it is replaced with another called Widdles. Sally describes her love for native animals and her nursing of a baby mudlark that dies unexpectedly. The swamp behind the house becomes the children's favourite haunt where they spend time catching gilgies. Gladys and Daisy become amateur meteorologists. Daisy begins to predict storms but unfortunately, without much precision.

Chapter Ten: Cure Alls

After the death of Dad, Mum, i.e. Gladys, becomes very religious and starts attending all churches. The children, however, start going to the Seventh Day Adventist Church because they show films about devils and angels. Sally narrates how she was a sickly child and how she recovered from rheumatic fever because of Nan's and Mum's nursing. Nan and Mum are obsessed with prevention of ill-health and Nan always uses old cures to prevent problems, cures like pepper on gashes and beetroot juice to replace loss of blood.

Chapter Eleven: Getting Ahead

Gladys gets a job as a school cleaner and the children, especially Sally, help her after school. The children now begin to have some extra treats like a visit to the Royal Show and marshmallows and the adults get to bet on the TAB. Nan is obsessed with bushfires and prepares for a fire that never takes place. Whenever there had been bushfires, she had refused to evacuate and had kept a number of men's handkerchiefs to cover faces with.

Sally becomes President of the Red Cross at school and has a successful year in Grade Six. Their Guy Fawkes Night is ruined by Nan and her fear of fire. The family's newly acquired dog, Tiger, is run over by a bus but generally, there is now no dearth of money. Nan begins to show Sally special things in the garden.

Chapter Twelve: Triumphs and Failures

When Sally is in Grade Seven, David starts going to school. He is a gentle boy who is always in trouble when interacting with his teacher who is a middle-aged spinster. Sally develops allergy to chalk and manages to get several half-days off school. The year, however, is eventful and Sally wins the Dick Cleaver Award for Citizenship.

Sally notices that when her friends visit Nan disappears. She is angry with Sally for bringing friends home for she is ashamed of how they live.

Sally does badly in the tests which decide whether one is to join the Professional stream or the Commercial one and Mum is very upset. Sally wants to study art in Paris and nothing else.

Chapter Thirteen: Growing Up

At school the children are warned about strangers and Sally realizes that not all people are trustworthy. An uncle makes sexual advances towards her and her sister but Sally foils his moves. However, she realizes that she is growing up: like with everyone, at puberty her skin becomes patchy.

Sally has her first argument with Nan over the futility of trying to sterilize the house with chopped onions. Nan discovered Medic spray instead and used it.

Fortunately for Sally, she makes it to the professional stream at school and Gladys is very happy. Jill begins attending school and adapts well. Helen begins primary school. Sally starts absenting herself from class for she says she hates regimentation and feels better after playing truant. Once when Mum picks them up in the car, they are caught and have to tell lies to save her.

Chapter Fourteen: Rather Peculiar Pets

Gladys is fond of stuffed pets as well as live ones. She picks up a new dog called 'Curly,' who keeps unwanted callers away. He is, however, excessively affectionate towards the Legatee and spills his tea with the result that the man now communicates only through the phone or through letters.

Chapter Fifteen: A Black Grandmother

After the currency changes in Australia in February 1966 from pound, shilling and pence to decimal currency, Gladys and Daisy hoard all the old money expressing their fear of governmental authority. Sally fails in her examinations in all but English and Art. Nan believes in her potential as an artist but Mum and her teacher do not and so, one day, she burns her work out of frustration.

One day, Sally comes home to find Nan crying that she was a Black grandmother and that the children want a White one. Jill realizes that they are Aboriginals and not Indians and finally tells Sally "we're Boongs!" (98). Sally then begins to pester her Mum and Nan to tell her more about their Aboriginal descent but she is warned about bothering Nan. For some time, Sally relegates her search for identity to the background and studies hard for her school-leaving and succeeds in passing with high marks in English and Art.

Chapter Sixteen: What People Are We?

In the fourth year, Sally joins the youth group and assists in organizing interesting activities for the young people but she is disillusioned when the Deacon of a church asks her to stop seeing his daughter as he believes that she is a bad influence on her. Her compliance, she feels, is born of her Mum and Nan's subservience to authority. She realizes that they are terrified of power and are afraid of declaring their Aboriginal origin.

Chapter Seventeen: Make Something of Yourself

In 1967 Mum buys a florist's shop with a loan from Lois. She wishes her children had been more ambitious but Sally has no drive. She begins to realize that her family is different. One day she hears her grandmother pretending to be a White when talking to the rentman.

As they get richer, Nan and Mum both become "avid collectaholics." Nan has collected lots of Adventist brochures for use as toilet paper in an emergency. Gladys has collected other things including tools that are never put to any use.

Sally works hard and passes her examinations but does not want to study again. Over a game of volleyball, Sally hears of a popular girl of another church who turns out to be a Black and is going to return to her people to help them.

Chapter Eighteen: The Working Life

In 1969 Sally begins to work as a clerk in a government department but soon starts finding feeling bored. She leaves this job and now finds work as a laboratory assistant. After a stint here, she decides to go to the University to study psychology.

Chapter Nineteen: Home Improvements

As the family becomes increasingly secure economically, the girls want more and more conveniences. They do not want to have their clothes boiled or burned by Nan's cigarettes. The old copper vessel for washing clothes is soon replaced by a twin-tub washing machine which Nan soon learns to use. A hot water system replaces the old-fashioned chip heater and there is an effort at wallpapering the lounge-room.

An elderly English friend of Sally called Cyril comes to stay for a night but remains there for six months. He offers to do odd jobs but he causes problems which outweigh the help extended by him. The loud classical music that he plays is deafening. He leaves when Nan rips his shirt off a rosebush at the front of the house.

Chapter Twenty: A New Career

Sally enjoys life in the University because of the relative freedom it gives; she also likes the reading and discussion on the campus. She supports herself on a Repatriation scholarship that she had been awarded.

Nan's eyesight begins to get impaired as a consequence of which she shoves a plate of dog food before Mum, mistaking her hair for the dog's. Mum buys her a pair of binoculars which enable her to see things clearly.

Sally struggles through her second year in Psychology. It is during these days that she meets Paul who is a teacher. When he visits them, Nan does not disappear because she feels that he is one of them. In the second term of her third year in the University, Sally gets engaged to Paul and the two decide to get married. David and Paul together work on the driveway of the Milroy house with gravel and a roller.

Chapter Twenty-One: Owning Up

Sally marries Paul Morgan on the ninth of December 1972. Aunt Vi, Mum's friend, and Mrs. Morgan come to help. Sally finds Nan crying because she feels that the children do not need her any more.

Sally wishes to change her major subject, in her degree course and thus has to repeat a year's study in Psychology. Sally and Paul move to South Perth into a crumbling house that is infested with rats. Nan has taught Sally things like lighting a fire, chopping wood, gutting a chicken for a meal, nursing sick animals etc., but none of these skills help her in the present situation. Jill soon moves in with them and then they discuss their Aboriginality and Mum's silence on the issue. However, Mum finally does admit to the girls that they are Aboriginals.

Chapter Twenty-Two: A Beginning

Sally, making a fresh beginning, applies for an Aboriginal scholarship, which she is awarded but she has to promise Nan not to tell the government anything about the latter. After this, Nan takes more interest in Black people and identifies herself as a *Nyoongah.*

Sally tells her friends about her Aboriginality but they do not believe her. She is reported to have cheated the Commonwealth Department of Education by falsely declaring herself to be an Aboriginal and has to defend herself before an official. However, she is able to keep the scholarship for losing it would have meant a denial of Nan's heritage.

Mum becomes more forthcoming with facts about Nan and her past. She tells Sally that Nan was born at Corunna Downs Station, which was owned by Drake Brockmans and that Nan was Judy's nurse-maid when the latter was a baby.

When Sally once calls the dog "a bloody mongrel," Nan's sensibility is violated and she is upset because she feels that Sally has abused a child. Perhaps, the Aboriginals were derogatively referred to as "bloody mongrels" in the past.

Chapter Twenty-Three: A Visitor

Sally graduates but continues studying at the Western Australian Institute of Technology. Helen remains the only one still at school for David completes his school-leaving examinations.

Mum tells Sally that her father was a White man who died when she was very young but she does not know his name and identity.

In 1975 Sally is blessed with a daughter called Ambelin Star. Nan is becoming more difficult to get along with because of her increasing sense of never having been loved. In 1978 Sally's son is born. Nan's brother, Arthur, starts visiting the family frequently. Nan and Arthur argue in their own language over little things and the latter threatens to tell Sally her Aboriginal name. Later, Nan teaches Sally some words of their Aboriginal language.

Chapter Twenty-Four: Where There's a Will

In 1979 Sally decides to write a book about her family heritage. She buys a typewriter and learns to type. She begins to research in Aboriginal history, especially their past in Western Australia. She acquires the birth certificate of her Mum, who was born in King Edward Memorial Hospital which was unusual for an Aboriginal child. Significant facts like the name of Mum's father are, however, not mentioned on the certificate.

Sally goes to visit Aunt Judy at Cottesloe who was Nan's employer at Corunna Downs. She agrees to disclose facts about Nan. She says that Nan's father was Maltese Sam, the cook at Corunna Downs Station, and that Mum's father was Jack Grime, who had no other children and spent most of his life in Sidney. She says Mum liked him and he used to visit her in the florist's shop. Mainly, what is relevant here is that the Drake-Brockman family is linked to them somehow. Sally gets information that takes her to Judy's mother, old Aunt Alice in Wollongong in New South Wales.

Arthur is well informed about life at Corunna Station because he has spent several years of his life there. There is, however, a conflict of versions and the secret of Nan's birth remains unravelled for there are no records kept for Aboriginals and nothing can be verified.

Chapter Twenty Five: Part of Our History

Sally is unable to elicit further information from Nan. Her mother promises to try getting more facts out of Nan and does succeed to a great extent. She learns that Howden Drake-Brockman was Nan's father. Nan quarrels with Arthur about not wanting to name people. The latter enquires about the book Sally is writing and agrees to tell his story.

Arthur visits the Milroys several times in the next three years. He repeatedly refers to Nan as an ignorant blackfella because she cannot read and write as he can. This upsets Nan.

Sally dreams that Arthur is going to die and realizes that this is why he is working hard on his story. Paul minds the children when Sally is busy recording Arthur's story. After three months, Arthur decides to go back to Mucka to die on his own land. He says, with a sense of belonging and identity, that he is "yearning for that place. My own home, my land. I been away too long. Can you understand that?" (164)

Chapter Twenty Six: Links with the Past

In 1982 when Sally is carrying her third child, she goes to Sidney to visit Alice Drake-Brockman who was living in a nursing home in Wollongong. Alice says that Daisy's father was Maltese Sam, the alcoholic younger son of an affluent family and a profligate. Daisy's mother, Annie, was a dress maker and it was she who had asked Alice to take Daisy away. Alice was prosecuted as it was unlawful to take Aboriginal girls to Perth. After winning the case, however, she brought in other girls as well. She went back to Corunna Downs only once when it was sold and the family bought another place called Towera Station nine hundred miles away. In the course of her exploration of the past, Sally finds out that her Mum had lived in Parkerville, a home run by the sisters of the Church of England. She comes back to the West to have a holiday. Arthur dies while she is there and the entire family except Nan is able to attend the funeral.

Alice had been nice to the family. It was she who had driven Daisy to the hospital when she delivered Gladys. She had later organized for Gladys to be placed at Parkerville. Also she had helped Gladys obtain a florist's apprenticeship though this was a cognizable offence under law. When Sally later asks Mum about Parkerville, she is not very forthcoming about any kind of information. Sally then begins to work on Arthur Corunna's story.

Arthur Corunna's Story (c1893-c1950)

Arthur's life is traced through a series of stories narrated to Sally. He starts with an introduction to his parents and to what we know as his 'place.' He says he has two fathers, one White, Howden Drake-Brockman and one Aboriginal, who was a boolyah man who frightened others. He talks of how he got a sense of place from the days he spent on the Station after which he was taken to the Swan Native and Half-Caste Mission on the Swan River where he was christened Corunna. Eventually, however, he boards a train to run away to the goldfields leaving his brother, Albert, there, for the Mission was like a jail where the children were called inmates and were harried by bullies and discriminated against.

Arthur soon gets station work with a man called Mc Quarie. After Mc Quarie's business collapses, he works first with a man called Hancock and then with Davy Jones. He makes enough money from these ventures to be able to buy a farm at Muckinbudin. Having acquired prosperity, he desires to bring Daisy home from Ivanhoe, where she is working as a servant at the Drake-Brockmans, to marry a friend of his but things do not work out as Daisy is pregnant and gives birth to a child in 1927.

At this time, Arthur takes to boxing and wrestling and tells Sally some stories related to this part of his life. In the early Thirties, he marries Adeline Wilkis in a Catholic Church by picking her name out of a hat three times in a row. After that he survives the Depression and trouble with neighbours. He narrates the ordeals and injustices associated with being Aboriginals.

Arthur has three sons and a daughter and generally, he thinks that he has had a good life, but feels that the quality of his life would have been very different if he had really been a White for he is often mistaken for one.

Chapter Twenty Seven: Where to Next?

Sally plans a second visit to Corunna Downs so as to be able to explore her past further. She wants her Mum to accompany her but Mum and Nan are both opposed to this. Mum, however, finally joins the children in heading off North. Sally carries a video camera for recording things.

Chapter Twenty Eight: Return to Corunna

At Port Hedland Sally meets Jack McPhee, who is a friend of Albert Brockman and through his 'blackfella' relationships, a cousin of Nan. Jack provides Sally and Mum with a lot of information regarding people and places. Born in 1903, he worked in Corunna Downs from 1924 onwards and remembers that Maltese Sam is not Daisy's father. He also remembers taking a pregnant Daisy from Hillside to Corunna in 1923.

Fortunately, Sally and Mum get to Marble Bar on pension day and are able to meet a lot of people. They interact with a number of locals and with the information collected are able to piece together a lot of their historical past as Aboriginals. An interpreter, Gladys Lee, accompanies them to the Reserve, where they come across Topsy and Nancy who are like an extended family. After this they move to Corunna Downs which is now devoid of any Aboriginals but it is still very beautiful – they see the kitchen, shed, tank machine and the soft blue hills. Their guide, Doris, gives them a grinding stone for Nan. It is now that they have a sense of place and feel complete as a people who know their place. Sally now wants Nan to change and accept her past without reservations.

Chapter Twenty Nine: Someone like Me

Nan is happy to see them back home and watches the video film they had made of Corunna Downs with interest and a sense of nostalgia. She talks about Lily and is surprised to learn that Topsy and Nancy are still alive.

Sally enquires of her mother again as to who the latter's father was. When Gladys was a child she thought Jack Grime was her father but a comparison of her photograph with Jack Grime's reveals that they did not look alike. In fact, there was more of a resemblance between her and Howden. Questions about Gladys' missing sister upset Nan.

Gladys Corunna's Story (1931-1983)

At Sally's insistence, Gladys finally agrees to tell her story. She says that she does not really remember the time when she went to Parkerville Children's Home at the age of three but generally speaking she had a difficult time there. She suffered and had to work hard but she had some happy times, too. One major incident that she remembers is when she was taken to Ivanhoe in Perth to see her mother who was very seriously ill. The latter was on the verge of death after having given blood to save her own sister.

Gladys often went to Ivanhoe during her holidays to see her Mum. She recounts how difficult things were during the Depression of the 1930s. Gladys says that she was not particularly fond of school but had some good times there like the annual trip to the pictures and the holiday she spent at the beach at Cottesloe.

Later, when Gladys' mother was asked to leave Ivanhoe, she started working for the Morgans but after two years, Gladys tells us, she went back to Ivanhoe because she was offered a lifetime job there. However, Daisy lived a hard life there and when she brought Gladys home, the latter was not allowed to live there. Gladys was sent to the Hewitts and Daisy was again asked to leave. Finally the two were reunited when they started living together in a rented accommodation at Molly Skinner's house.

Gladys finished school at the age of sixteen in 1943. As it was not possible for her to go to a business college like her friends, she first worked in a restaurant and then Alice got her a job at the florist's in Claremont where her remuneration was six shillings a week. What worried Daisy then was her going out with American soldiers. Daisy and Gladys soon took alternative accommodation and the former told the latter never to admit being an Aboriginal for that would have terrible consequences.

Gladys met Bill at a party and started dreaming about him and their relationship. Daisy did not approve of Bill because of his addiction to liquor but Gladys finally married him in a registry office when she was twenty-one. She had told him that she was an Aboriginal before getting married but he had not then reacted in any way though his parents had disapproved of the alliance.

Gladys and Bill lived with Daisy after they got married and Gladys continued to work for the florist. When Sally was born, they shifted to a tradesman's flat at Beaconsfield. Sally was very seriously ill several times, but Gladys believed that she saw the figure of a nun next to her cot. Bill was with the 2/16 Battalion but after he was wounded he was sent to the Middle East. Later he was shipped to Italy and then tortured by the Italian police. Later, he went through a series of humiliating experiences during war but he never told Gladys the whole story though she knew he had been degraded.

When the next child, Jill, was born, Gladys nearly died. Bill had a nervous breakdown and was admitted to Hollywood Hospital where he lived in a dream world. When Billy was born, everyone believed that a golden angel hovered over Gladys. Then came David who was a breach baby. Bill had been given State Housing in Manning where the children had place to play. Gladys and Daisy could hear spirit corroborees there until Bill died. When Bill was in hospital for a full year Gladys attended spiritualist meetings where she became a healer.

In April 1959 Helen was born and then one night in October 1960 when Bill seemed to be much better, he died. Gladys was so shocked that a neighbour had to tell the children of Bill's death. Gladys had a vision of Bill happy in a garden in the company of other people.

Gladys received a war pension which eased out her financial problems. She and Daisy decided not to tell the children that they were Aboriginal. Daisy was secure having a home with Gladys and her grandchildren.

Gladys, in having bought a florist's shop, now experiences a sense of independence and pride and regrets the fact that she ever wanted to be a White. She is proud of her children and her heritage. She ends her story by saying that it was not easy narrating the incidents of her past life.

Chapter Thirty: Something Serious

Daisy is admitted to the hospital with an infected and collapsed lung. While she is in bed, Sally reads to her Arthur's boxing story. Though exhausted and out of breath, Daisy describes Corunna Downs as she knew it.

Helen is doing her residency in the hospital that Daisy is in and this facilitates their getting the latter's reports early. Daisy is diagnosed as having a malignant tumour and there seems to be a danger of septicemia resulting from the malignancy. The registrars in the hospital use Daisy as a patient in a practice-examination. Sally protests and wants to complain but Gladys prevents her from doing so as Helen has yet to finish her course.

Chapter Thirty One: Good News

Sally cleans the sleepout in her home so that Daisy can stay with her and go home only for the weekends. Daisy enjoys staying with Sally's children, Amber and Blaze, and exchanges stories with them. When Sally and Daisy get talking about the past, Daisy agrees to tell her story but lays the condition that she would maintain secrecy about certain things including facts about her sister.

Daisy Corunna's Story: 1900-1983

Daisy begins her story by telling Sally how she was born under a gum tree and delivered by an Aboriginal midwife while the children of the tribe witnessed her birth. Daisy's Aboriginal name is Talahue. Her surname was first Brockman and later became Corunna. She did not know about Maltese Sam but she knew that her Aboriginal father was Chinaman. She had two full-blooded sisters. She was close to Rosie who died at an early age. Her mother had cried when Arthur had been sent away from her. Albert was light-skinned. Since he got sick when he was taken away from home, he was sent back. Daisy's skin became lighter with the passage of time and she was afraid that her White blood would subdue her black blood.

As Daisy grew older, she was made to work in the main house and sleep in the verandah. At the age of fourteen or fifteen, she was taken away from her mother but then she thought she was going to school and would come back. Actually, she was sent to Perth to work for the Drake-Brockmans there. Nell Drake-Brockman had been very cruel to her and she had not even been given a bed.

When the family moved to Ivanhoe, Daisy had a lot of work to do and was Nanny to five children. She was treated like a servant and missed her own people. Her only friend was Mrs. Quigley at Claremont.

Daisy never liked Perth then and .she tells Sally about the discrimination, humiliation and sexual harassment that she underwent there. Arthur was her only support and that too the Whites took away from her. Gladys, she says, was separated from her when the former was only three. She elaborates nostalgically on the time she and Gladys had spent together before her daughter married Bill, who called her a "bloody nigger." Daisy never really cared for Bill but says that it was the war that made him what he was. Once when Gladys had polio Daisy moved in with her and used her special powers to heal Gladys. She calls Bill's parents "mongrels" for they never helped Gladys after Bill died.

Daisy refuses to tell Sally anything more. She says that she is looking forward to meeting Arthur in her next life. She says that she does not trust the Government and that she wants the Government and the White people to admit their mistakes. Aboriginal people, she says, are not owned any more. She also states that the Black people need to leave drinking alcohol. She thinks it would be good to be respected like the Whites and treated honourably like them.

Chapter Thirty Two: The Bird Call

Daisy winds up her tale but Sally knows the Nan has not divulged everything to her yet, Sally is happy that her grandmother has broken her silence and has told her at least something about her past. She also observes that Nan's language had changed when she narrated her story of her past days. While Sally helps Nan undress, the latter tells her about how the treatment meted out to her was like that given to a beast and how she was referred to as a dirty old blackfella.

Daisy goes to Gladys' place where her condition worsens and she is confined to bed. Sally too is sick due to emotional exhaustion. The next morning Jill rings her to tell her that she had heard the bird call which symbolizes the coming of death. Daisy is taken to the hospital and dies there at 7 a.m. Sally too hears the bird call now.

My Place: The Setting

The setting of *My Place* in Australia is an important part of the text. With reference to the country's historical background the work explores Australia's attitude towards and its treatment of its native people. Sally's persistent efforts at unearthing her past and adopting that past with a sense of pride and dignity show her focused motivation in asserting her identity as an Aboriginal.

The contextual relationship between the Aboriginal people and their land has a special significance in life for Aboriginal culture presupposes that the inhabitants of a place are an integral part of the land. Identity is firmly linked to the place one lives in and those Aborigines who are not in contact with their land lose their personal and tribal individuality. When the Europeans came to live in Australia as one of their colonies, they failed to comprehend this inherent and deep interrelationship between the people and their land. They evicted the tribals from their homes and transferred them to the reserves without thinking of the emotional turmoil caused to the latter by this act of dispossessing them of their land, and consequently of their identity and culture. A return to their land in search of identity is a major issue with the Aboriginals of the present times.

Corunna Downs station is an integral part of the historical past of the protagonist's family. Two generations of children were born here and their White fathers had a direct connection with this place. It is here that Gladys becomes conscious of the beauty of her country and of her indestructible bond with it. This eternal link is clearly visible in the fact that Arthur wants to go home to be able to die peacefully for it is there that he truly belongs.

The Pilbara region stretches from Port Hedland and Exmouth Gulf to the Northern Territory and is demarcated in the North by the De Grey river and in the South by the Ashburton river system. Corunna Downs station, which is the most significant locale in *My Place*, is in this region and lies mid-way between Marble Bar and Nullagine. It is a picturesque and beautiful place surrounded by low blue hills. In the beginning of the twentieth century, the station was owned by the Drake-Brockman family but it was actually the local tribe that contributed markedly in building up the station. This is corroborated by Arthur Corunna's report. In Sally Morgan's second work, *Wanamurraganya*, there are illustrations of Corunna Downs Station acquired from the Battye Library.

Other places of the Pilbara region referred to and described in *My Place* are Port Hedland, Marble Bar, Yandearra and Mukinbudin. Port Hedland, situated on a tidal island and joined to the coast by a causeway, is the main port for the Pilbara area. Marble Bar, initially the centre of the gold mining industry in the region, was linked to Port Hedland by rail. It is known to be the hottest place in Australia.

The low wages given to the Aboriginals in the Pilbara region triggered off the first Aboriginal strike in 1945. As Christian missions had not been allowed to enter the area by station owners, certain tribal groups were still unsevered and complete. By the year 1949, the Pindan movement initiated by the Aborigines, registered the Northern Development and Mining Company which built houses, drove trucks and carried guns and explosives. Ultimately they bought Yandearra station which was made to function on a communal basis.

Mukinbudin is a small town which is situated north-west of Perth. Arthur Corunna bought a farm in this town and came to be accepted as a White man. Evidently there was support for the Aboriginals in this district and they were evaluated on their merit.

My Place also gives us pieces of information about Perth from 1914 till the 1980s. Earlier, this city, situated on the banks of the Swan River was surrounded by marshes but the twentieth century witnessed several reclamation projects resulting in the building of parks, gardens and recreational areas. The rail link from Perth to Fremantle was extended to Guildford in 1881. Fremantle is a heavy industrial area.

The four main areas of Perth referred to in the text are Claremont, an inner suburb on Freshwater Bay close to the ocean, Parkerville situated to the east of the main city, Cottesloe, a beachside suburb near Claremont and Manning, flanked by the Canning River on two sides. Each of these places is of relevance to the text. The Drake-Brockmans owned the house called Ivanhoe in Claremont and Daisy worked there for many years. The Home Gladys was sent to when separated from Daisy was in Parkerville. A house at Cottesloe owned by the mission was the place where Gladys was sent for her holidays when the Drake-Brockmans refused to keep her one Christman. Manning was the suburb where the Milroys went to live in the 1950s and where Daisy and Gladys could hear spirit corroborees in the swamp at the back of the house. They firmly believed that this was essentially Aboriginal land. Here, each member of the family remained in contact with nature in different ways. Daisy always urged Sally and the others to be kind to natural things. Gladys had innumerable pets and the children loved the swamp adjoining the house. The weather forecasting story and Daisy's tree tapping to see if the plants were healthy are instances of excursions into nature.

My Place is a work that foregrounds the fact that the Aboriginal sense of place is central to the life of the Aborigines in Australia, essential for their very survival. The locating of their land by Sally and Gladys brings inconceivable joy to them and provides them a sense of belonging that they had never before experienced. Setting and place are thus vital to the text. The dedication of the book to her family and the epigraph expressing her sense of belonging to her tribal community are an epitome of the author's consciousness of being an integral part of her people and their "place" and her love for her own spiritual, cultural and ethnic roots:

> How deprived we would have been if we had been willing to let things stay as they were. We would have survived but not as a whole people, we would never have known our place.

My Place: The Characters

Our assessment of the major characters of *My Place* can only be based on the information provided to us by Sally Morgan herself. The work is not a piece of fiction and many of the individuals referred to in the book are still alive. Hence, these persons cannot strictly be called "characters" but as the writer has chosen to withhold some information regarding the various members of her family for reasons of privacy and we can never be fully acquainted with these people, we may, for academic purpose, speak of them as "characters."

Sally Morgan

Sally Morgan is the narrator-protagonist of her text who delineates here the various stages of the story of her discovery of her heritage and identity. She depicts herself as a person who was unaware of her rich heritage in her early life and then discovers her essential self and identity as an Aboriginal. The public image that she projects of herself as a member of the tribal community comes forth as an authentic one as she has discriminatingly chosen those convincing details of her life which lead us on to identify her with her tribe. Morgan often uses her sister, Jill, as an authorial voice to acquaint us with the different aspects of her personality and tell us how simple and naïve she was as a young girl.

Sally grew up in a new suburb in Perth in the 1950s and soon came to accept her Indian heritage. She went to the local primary school but resented the restrictions placed on her by government institutions. She was a keen observer of wildlife and enjoyed the swamp behind their house. Theirs was a close-knit family but her father, after the nervous breakdown caused by the traumatic experiences of war took to heavy drinking and had to be hospitalised very frequently. Eventually when he died, his children were very sad but relieved of the tension and poverty for which he was largely responsible.

Sally attended high school and wished to continue her studies but she often played truant from school, sometimes with the consent of her mother. She left school and worked for a year and then began University studies in psychology. To pass, Sally learned her lessons by heart. It is during this time that she met Paul and married him in 1972 after which she moved into another house. This made Gladys sad but the fact that Sally visited her family regularly kept her satisfied.

It was during one of these visits that Gladys finally told Sally about their Aboriginal roots, a fact she had been concealing till now for fear of her children being discriminated against. Sally promptly put in an application for an Aboriginal scholarship. It was an act which spoke of an assertion of her own identity as well as a social acceptance of it. When she was charged by the Commonwealth Department of Education of fraudulence, she found it outrageous. Such problems frequently recurred in Morgan's life and all because of her mother and grandmother's inability to fight back undue repression by authority.

Sally's family grew with the addition of three children between 1975 and 1982. She, however, continued to study as well. In 1979, Arthur Corunna started visiting Daisy and talking about the past. This inspired Sally to start writing a book on her family history for which he did some research on Aboriginal history in the Battye Library. She collected information regarding the past from the various relatives that she met. 'Auntie' Judy told her that Jack Grime was Gladys's father and Maltese Sam was

Daisy's father. Arthur Corunna too narrated his story and Sally recorded it.

In 1983 Sally returned to the Pilbara region with her husband, Paul, her children and Gladys. This time she collected bits of information about her great-grandmother, her grandmother and her great aunt. On visiting Corunna Downs itself, she experienced a sense of place that she had never felt before. With an understanding of and an insight into Daisy's bitterness, she now felt a complete person. She and Gladys both felt they belonged and they wanted Daisy to feel the same.

Later, Gladys gave Sally her account of what had happened to her in the past and it took the latter several months to record her story after the completion of which they discovered that Daisy was suffering from lung cancer. At this time Daisy moved in with Sally and went to Gladys only for weekends. It was during the time spent together that Sally managed to convince Daisy to relate her version of the past. Daisy, however, held back what she did not wish to divulge. Eventually, when Daisy died, both Jill and Sally heard the bird call her and this confirmed their Aboriginal descent.

Sally's quest in this work is depicted in the context of her everyday life, education, work, marriage and motherhood. It was only as a consequence of her persistent efforts at eliciting information from the various members of her family that Sally was able to give us a coherent rendering of her family history. She changed roles and modes to bring together a coherent and viable text with respect, accuracy and sensitivity. It is to her credit that she maintained a delicate balance between protecting her family and respecting its right to privacy and exposing it for a larger cause, that of creating links of empathy and oneness to bring together a now self-assertive community.

Daisy Corunna

It is Daisy's persistent denial of the Aboriginality of her family that gives Sally Morgan the determination to unearth her own identity and assert herself as a respectable member of the society despite the fact that she is an Aboriginal. Daisy, the diffident tribal characterized by submission to humiliation and discrimination is, two generations later, replaced by the confident Sally who proudly announces her Aboriginality to people around.

Daisy Brockman grew up on the Corunna Downs station in the Pilbara region of Western Australia but her name was later changed to Daisy Corunna. Arthur was Daisy's brother and visited her sometimes. They enjoyed each other's company but Daisy often fought with Arthur over the issue of their Aboriginality. Daisy lived her life in conformity with her parentage, the policy of removal and the prevalent Aboriginal Protection Act. The Australian law and her White family together denied her the pleasure of growing up within her family and of entering wedlock to savour a family of her own. She was made to live like a servant bearing children to her White masters and these children, as was customary, were removed from her after a particular age. However, Daisy loved her daughter and grandchildren and protected them in every way from indignities and humiliations.

Gladys Corunna

Daisy gave birth to Gladys in a Perth hospital and then presented her to Howden Drake-Brockman. When Gladys was three, the Drake-Brockmans expressed their inability to keep her and so Gladys was sent to a Children's Home at Parkerville. She was, however, able to spend her vacations with her mother at Ivanhoe in Perth. But, when she was twelve, the family refused to let her come even for Christmas. Ultimately, it was Daisy who moved out of the Drake-Brockmans' household to be with Gladys, who, after completing her high school started working as a florist. Much against the wishes of her mother, she married Bill Milroy in 1948 and initially they stayed with Daisy. When they got married, Bill had said that her being an Aboriginal did not matter to him but later he did seem to mind and became increasingly difficult to cope with. In the beginning Gladys had not realized that Bill had gone through traumatic experiences during war and his addiction to liquor was a consequence of the trauma he suffered. He died in 1960 entitling Gladys to receive a war pension. Gladys displayed great will power and tenacity of purpose in giving her children the best possible in life and in setting up her own florist's shop. She was a practising Christian and saw visions. During childbirth, she had the vision of an angel and before Bill's death she had a vision of Jesus. Though severed from the tribal land and culture, like her mother she also had visions of the corroborees in the swamp.

The visit to the Pilbara region with Sally was Gladys' first contact with her ancestral land and people and it gave her a sense of belonging. After this trip, she shed off her inhibitions and told Sally the story of her past days without keeping much back. She never complained about her Parkerville days and other harrowing experiences. She was a dutiful daughter who respected her mother's wishes till the very end when her mother wanted to die in hospital.

Bill Milory

Bill grew up in a family where there was little of discipline and where he was encouraged to start drinking at an early age. At fourteen he ran away from home to become a stockman. During the war, he changed Battalions and had several grilling experiences. Finally, as the Russians advanced in war, the prisoners were forced to march to Duderstadt and were liberated by the

Americans. They were, however, malnourished and Bill spent six months in an English hospital before he came home.

In 1948 he married Gladys and took up work as a plumber. His addiction to liquor, however, caused him to be hospitalised frequently and there was a progressive deterioration in his health. He could not look after his older children when Gladys went to hospital for childbirth next. Besides, his parents rejected Gladys and his children and he could not stand up to them.

Bill's condition worsened after the arrival of Frank Potter in Manning for the latter reminded him of his suffering and also encouraged him to drink. He had frequent nightmares and hallucinations and often became violent, at times assaulting Gladys too. He, however, did not respond to treatment and eventually committed suicide. Gladys received a war pension now but before this there was no help from any quarter.

All the information provided about Bill in the text makes him out to be a touchy and sensitive man emotionally shattered by what he underwent during war and even after the war days. He could never really share his war experiences fully with anybody, not even Gladys. He remained till the end an isolated man who could never forget the humiliation he suffered in the POW camps.

Arthur Corunna

Arthur was born in Corunna Downs station in about 1893, Earlier, like Daisy, he carried the surname Brockman but later became Corunna. He refused to change his name back to Brockman as he felt that his father had done nothing for him.

Arthur had a half-brother called Albert with whom he spent considerable time trying to learn the customs of the White people. Despite the fact that Arthur had an Aboriginal father, he never wanted to be a member of the tribe, happy only to share in the corroborees. When he was about twelve, Arthur along with

Albert and Katie was sent to Swan Native and Half Caste Mission in Fremantle. The man who looked after the mission treated the boys very cruelly and so Arthur and two other boys ran away from there with the help of some White people. Arthur, being a good worker, found employment easily and worked for various White people. Eventually he was able to earn enough money and buy a farm for himself. Unfortunately, he lost the farm in the Depression but he started work again on uncleared land and diligence paid dividends. All through Arthur was considered to be a White man and people had great regard for him as he was known to be a man of integrity in the business community.

Arthur was fond of Daisy and visited her frequently in Perth. He had a wife and four children but never very emotionally involved with them perhaps because of the experience of his own father never acknowledging him as his child. He was fond of Daisy and liked teasing her by calling her a "blackfella." He conceded to Sally's request of narrating his story to her because he wanted to be part of history.

Alice Drake-Brockman

Alice was the second wife of Howden Drake-Brockman. She married him in 1915 and settled down with him at Ivanhoe in Perth. She had two daughters by Howden, June and Judy and Daisy was called over from Corunna Downs to be their Nanny. She fought and won a legal battle to regularize Daisy's staying in Perth for as an Aboriginal she was not allowed to live in a town. Alice treated Daisy like a member of the family but when Daisy became pregnant she had to go back to Corunna Downs to deliver a baby girl. After her return to Ivanhoe, she again conceived and this time Alice drove her to the midwifery hospital where they could not refuse to admit her and Gladys was born. Gladys remained with Daisy till she was three. Much later in life,

Alice illegally obtained for Gladys a florist's apprenticeship when she left school.

Alice told Sally that Daisy's father was possibly Maltese Sam but that she did not know who Gladys's father was. Perhaps, she did not also know that Howden was the father of Arthur and Daisy as they lived at Corunna Downs after she got married.

Alice represents a blend of the old world attitude towards servants believing in being strict and severe with them and protests against unreasonable and biased laws. There was never, however, any report of Alice being cruel and inhuman in her treatment of servants. Rather, she often went out of her way to help them.

Jill Milroy

Jill, Sally's only sister, is her friend and confidante throughout the work and being only a year younger, attended school about the same time as Sally. Though Jill was far more pragmatic in her approach to problems than her sister, it was mostly the latter who was sent to manage and negotiate with their father when he was in a drunken state. When the fact of their being Aboriginals was revealed to Sally she discussed the issue with Jill who said that she already knew about it. So Sally was generally in a dream world whereas Jill was more practical. The Milroys had been a close-knit family and Jill and Sally had been good friends till Sally got married and became preoccupied with her own husband and children.

My Place: Themes

The major issues that emanate from the narrative determine the themes and ideas that prevail in the text. *My Place* deals primarily with the personal themes of family and identity with special reference to the Aboriginals of Australia but emerging from these matters in question arise certain social themes that become almost equally central to the work. Problems related to employment, removal, education, land rights, citizenship, reconciliation and addiction to alcohol assume significance when considered in the light of the specific historical background relating to the Aborigines in Australia.

In the late nineteenth and early and mid-twentieth century, European employers, especially the station owners and managers, treated the Australian Aboriginal people as their slaves. The Drake-Brockman family treated Daisy in this shoddy and cruel manner. From the age of twelve, she was made to work in the main house at Corunna Downs as a domestic servant and at fifteen the family took her to Ivanhoe to work as a Nanny and cook. To remain in the service of the family, Daisy was made to give up her child at the age of three, and of course, she was not allowed to get married and was never given any leave. When the family came to face a financial crisis, her services were terminated and she was not given any pay for her past services. The Drake-Brockmans paid only the Protection Board five shillings a year to avail themselves of Daisy's services. This was a common story for other Aboriginal women as well.

Arthur Corunna had better luck than his sister for when he escaped from the Home, he found people who paid him fairly for the work he did and thus he was able to consolidate his financial position. Most Aboriginal stockmen and labourers were paid in terms of food and sometimes clothing and station owners would not have been able to afford European labour to do the same work and thus Australia owes its development primarily to the availability of inexpensive Aboriginal labour.

The policies of the *Aboriginal Protection Act*, the *1936 Native Administration Act* and the policies of the *Board* under A.O. Neville had established the practice of the *removal* of children from Aboriginal mothers. It was believed that Aborigines would be assimilated better into White society if they were brought up in the company of White people.

Removal disintegrated Aboriginal communities and families leaving the separated children with no sense of identity or feeling of belonging to either their own original communities or to the White community they had been reared in. Gladys Corunna had been removed from her mother, Daisy, and sent to Parkerville Children's Home at the age of three. Though Gladys was never really ill-treated, she found the rules and regulations of the institution suffocating and she missed the affection of the elders that a child craves for. She was, however, able to come back to her mother at the age of fourteen. Like the other girls in the Home, Gladys, too, wanted to be like the White people but later she was ashamed of herself for ever having wanted to be White.

Under the *Protection Act* Aboriginal children were entitled to education only upto class three at a primary school so that they could just about read, write, add, subtract and multiply. The girls were specifically trained in domestic skills like cooking and sewing and the boys were taught the labouring skills so that by the age of fourteen, Aboriginal children were equipped to be domestic helps.

Daisy in *My Place* could not read or write at all as she had received no education. Arthur always complained that he had not been well-educated. Gladys had good skills but once again she was fortunate to have had a good teacher who encouraged her to read Shakespeare and to do Algebra. Gladys's education was sufficient for her to be able to manage her own business.

Sally, when appearing for her IQ test in school, faced the problem of cultural difference. Since the test had no relevance to the culture she had been exposed to, she did not fare well. What she studied in high school did not really interest her. She only liked Art and English but even there, her Art teacher mocked at her efforts and made fun of them.

Land rights in Australia are all based on the fact that the White colonists appropriated the land of the natives and settled there illegally though the Aboriginal people possessed prior proprietorial rights of the land. Arthur Corunna had over-ridden the tribal practices and had bought and developed his own land so that he could bequeath it to his children.

Another issue obliquely referred to in *My Place* is the question of citizenship. The 1967 Referendum gave the Aboriginals citizenship of Australia. Before this they were treated like animals and not counted in the national census. After 1967 Aboriginal people who wished to join the White community could be given on exemption certificate but then they could no longer receive any benefits from the *Protection Board*. They were, however, required to carry their exemption certificates with them and these certificates contained photographic identification but they were supposed to live outside the town premises and that is why Alice Drake-Brockman is said to have violated law in having brought Daisy to live in Perth.

Reconciliation, again, is an issue that has been indirectly addressed in *My Place*. The aim of the *Council for Aboriginal Reconciliation* since 1991 has been to encourage good will and understanding between Australians through the medium of education and communication. Daisy always felt that the Government and the White people should acknowledge the injustices they have meted out to the Aboriginals and make whatever amends were possible.

The personal themes taken up in *My Place* deal primarily with the issue of the erosion of Aboriginal identity through the policies of *removal* and *assimilation*. With the bar against speaking their own languages and practising their own traditions and customs, the Aboriginals are left with no sense of cultural and personal individuality. It was only after Sally Morgan went to the Pilbara region to explore her tribal culture that she felt she was a complete person. She had previously been deprived of the link with her land and her people but now she was driven by an inner compulsion to discover the essential spirit of the Aboriginals. Sally was of the generation of the so-called "mission children" who wished to protest against the policy of *removal* and to reconstruct their past with the avowed purpose of reviving their rich heritage.

Although Gladys did not say it in as many words, she too discovered her true self after her trip north with Sally. She acquired a sense of belonging which was exhilarating and very satisfying. Daisy with her oppressive past felt differently. She never considered it a privilege to be an Aboriginal. In fact, she was ashamed of the fact that she was "a dirty old blackfella." To her Aboriginality meant pain and suffering but she was not to be blamed for she had gone through harrowing experiences which made her very uncertain regarding her future and the future of her children and grandchildren.

The significance and centrality of the family and the family bonds in the Aboriginal social framework cannot be denied. 'Family' is defined in terms of blood ties and marriages but culture and language also play an important role in defining kinship.

The Aboriginals, on the basis of kinship, are divided into 'skin' groups, each of which has its own guidelines and rules regarding conduct and marital alliances. Each group is again divided into two opposite parts called "moities" and these relate the members of the group to the universe and to their land. All groups are characterized by family closeness—physical and emotional. Daisy and Gladys had both been deprived of this kind of closeness but they ensured that their children were close enough to feel for each other.

Aboriginal society has exclusive rituals and social practices for men and women and a member of one sex is not allowed to attend the ceremonies and conventional practices of the other. In other words, the practices of women are not always made public and some of them are closely guarded secrets. We are told very little about Daisy's mother, Annie, except for the fact that she had an Aboriginal husband, a *boolya* man, and also bore Howden Drake-Brockman children. Daisy, though not initiated herself, knew that she had an Aboriginal mother. When Gladys was born, she gave her an initiation scar to protect her. Daisy, till the very end, kept some of her relationships to herself, never divulging them to any one.

Gladys did not have any tribal education but she, too, would have liked to keep many things private. Besides, she was shy of discussing women's issues like childbirth with Sally too but she finally overcame her hesitation. In narrating her story, she kept nothing back for she wanted to give her children their spiritual background through her own characteristic Aboriginal experiences.

Autobiography as Strategy of Resistance and Empowerment: Sally Morgan's *My Place*

REENA MITRA
Christ Church College, Kanpur

Sally Morgan, currently Director of the Centre for Indigenous History and the Arts at the University of Western Australia, is an author of repute and her published works include *My Place*, *Wanamurraganya*, several books for children and a play called *Sistergirl*. Her standing rests, in the main, on her magnum opus, *My Place*, for which she won the 1987 Australian Human Rights Award for Literature and the 1990 Order of Australia Book Prize. In addition to being a writer of consequence she is a gifted visual artist whose paintings express themes similar to those she explores in My Place—themes that spell out the importance of land and land rights, spirit life, political issues and the significance of birds and snakes. Arnold Oganov firmly believes that artistic creation "strives towards maximum sensory tangibility in artistic depiction"[1] and Morgan conforms to this by relying on her intense visual memory and photographic retention to record details that would ordinarily have been lost to aesthetic presentation.

Sally Morgan's narrative design provides art with an inexhaustible means of cognition and a grasp of the surrounding world with its socio-historical conditions which are major determinants of the form life takes at diverse points of time. The means and modes of cognition which her narrative method provides help us arrive at an aesthetic interpretation of reality or what is commonly referred to as artistic truth. "Artistic truth is life's truth aesthetically interpreted. . . . It is a result of cognition set down in a work of art."[2]

Australian literature, like all Commonwealth literatures, having navigated the passage-way from the station of a nascent literature in English with its beginnings in the bush ballads to the status of a literature that has attained its maturity and efflorescence, has now, a distinct identity of its own. Its creative writers have faced the particular challenge of adapting the English language to portray effectively the realities of their national spirit, life, culture and landscapes and to approximate "life's truth"[3] Thus, it is for them, essentially, a matter of adapting an alien language to the native spirit. In his Introduction to the *Collins Book of Australian Poetry*, Rodney Hall, referring to the revitalized use of English by the writers of the Jindy-Worobak Club in Adelaide, talks of their "rejecting English words too weighty with overtones foreign to Australia and replacing them by images that attempted some native strength."[4]

Australian literature today successfully reflects the national consciousness and spirit in its own distinctive idiom and imagery and its writers explore reality and value in Australia from a varied perspective—social, historical and individual. In reading the works of Australian writers, then, the many configurations evident in the relationship of these writers with their cultures become the focus of exploration and study. The enquiry that arises in the critical mind is with regard to how these authors convey this sense of belonging to their cultures within the matrix of their work. The answer to this query lies in the observation made by Pushpinder Syal in her assertion that "cultural contexts are not represented in a text, they are mediated by the writers' perceptions and purposes and hence by the language used."[5] In the context of creative writing in Australia, the work is a record of the ever-evolving process of negotiation between the writer and the community.

Women writers of Australia have instituted a characteristic convention by writing about aspects and concerns different from those chosen by men. The body of their works is markedly distinct and presents an alternative view of the culture and customs of the country. Letter writing was the initial activity of White women that encouraged them to venture into literary creative compositions marked by introspection and the urge to self-development. The voice of "exile" is another unmistakable feature of Australian women's writings which seek to establish the identity of womankind and to re-constitute the prevailing value so as to make them relevant to the intensifying feminist assertions and acceptable in the postcolonial context.

Sally Morgan, a writer of singular personal power, writes perceptively of themes and characters from Australia's past. She defines the postcolonial consciousness in terms of alienation and the death of the native culture of the place which was slowly marginalized and uprooted. She draws our attention to the spiritual mystery of human life and relationships. Most importantly, though she herself was only part aboriginal, Sally Morgan was a vocal champion of the Australian Aborigines, whose land, she believed, had been appropriated by the Whites. Her love for the countryside, her "blood's country," makes her identify herself with the pristine Australian psyche that existed before the influx of the Whites from England. The White man, as C.D. Narasimhaiah puts it, "has committed a 'bloodless murder' of the aborigine but here is more evidence of real attrition of the heart for what has happened to the primitive man than elsewhere."[6]

Sally Morgan, through her works, has helped to sensitize the society she lives in to the plight of the Aborigines, who did not, like the Red Indians, resist "invasion" and put up a fight against the colonists; they just withdrew into the outbacks to be at peace with themselves. Judith Wright's poem, "Nigger's Leap" speaks of the "silent wounds of Australian history"[7] caused by the effacement and extirpation of the Aborigines by the White men. These "silent wounds" inflicted upon the Aborigines are registered in the works of several Australian writers. "Literature," it is believed, records the path traversed, it unfolds a motley canvas of history in the wake of the moving masses."[8] A serious writer, however, not only records facts and events but also pronounces a verdict in conformity with his own understanding of life and truth which help him distil historically significant phenomena. The Aboriginal writers took it upon themselves to rewrite their past with the express purpose of strengthening the Native readers' sense of identity.

Sally Morgan's *My Place* belongs to the bulk of Australian women's writing and has the distinction of being the first Aboriginal narrative of exposé, a public statement of the shocking facts of racial, cultural and political domination of the Whites over the Natives. The work is a poignant tale of marginalisation, alienation and the diaspora experience. The themes explored in it are those of racial discrimination, Aboriginal identity, feminist assertion and class and gender concerns. Victoria Laurie clearly defines the thematic contents of the work: "Morgan's *My Place* is the picture of generational dispossession and denial of land, of kinship, of successive children stolen away, of wealthy White men, who disowned them . . . an account of how she cajoled and gently bullied her family towards the truth about their collective Aboriginal identity."[9]

The prevailing spirit in Sally Morgan's work is that of the recreation of the Australian landscape, its people and its history as it is in other specimens of Aboriginal writing in English like the works of Mudrooroo and Archie Weller and prose writers like Alice Nannup, Ruby Langford Ginibi, Oodgeroo, Noonuccal and Kevin Gilbert. Ronald Berndt traces, in the endeavours of Aboriginal writers, "the emergence of a literature which will be the underpinning of a newly conceived Aboriginal heritage. . . . It is a heritage which is now both traditional and mixed with the traumatic circumstances of the struggle of a people to find or to assert their own unique identity, and have that identity recognized by others."[10]

Biography and autobiography form a substantial part of Native writing as Natives feel the urge to write about their place, their people and their times. In terms of their autobiographical narratives the status of the Australian Aboriginals is a peculiar one because they have been marginalized and pushed to the psychic and political brink of a society comprising a group of people who have themselves been subjected to colonial atrocities and persecution.

Augustine's memoirs, *Confessions*, written between 397 and 400 AD, established the convention of converting experience into narrative, life into textual self-representation. Such an exercise is termed an autobiography. The autobiographical process is a recreation of the author's personality, which is seen in retrospect. This artistic activity helps the autobiographer in determining his true identity and enables him to etch out an accurate picture of himself. The self-referentiality of autobiography is also self-interrogative and thus, a work beginning in self-depiction ends in a deeper knowledge of the self. "Self-portraiture . . . is a synonym of self-knowledge."[11]

My Place records the reminiscences of Sally Morgan and a historiographic depiction of the traumatic experiences in the lives of her kinsmen. An absorbing series of incidents unravels the enigmatic facts of the Aboriginal identity of Sally's ancestry. The chronicle demonstrates the circumstances under which the Aborigines still continue to define themselves in terms of black/ White confrontation and are aware of themselves only as they stand in relation to the dominant White culture. The ray of hope lies in the fact that they appear to be gradually moving towards an assertion of their native identity.

The autobiographical stance chosen by Sally Morgan in *My Place* is clearly a strategy for the expression of a growing defiance and insubmissiveness on the part of the Aborigines. The work, like other autobiographies of Aboriginal women, is an implicit campaign for registering resistance and seeking empowerment. Morgan reinforces in her book the view that gender constructs are created by men and that women are branded by them as mere instruments of procreation. A woman, thus, assessed in terms of sexual commerce, is further devalued if she happens to be an Aboriginal. Nan and Gladys, we are told, have both been subjected to this kind of humiliation; they prefer to leave their past buried and to conceal their Aboriginal origin. Gladys peremptorily tells Sally, "There's no point in digging up the past, some things are better left buried."[12] All enquiries regarding descent and nationality thus continue to be responded to with the word, "Indian." It is only as we trace the denouement of the work that we see how the substitution of "Aboriginal" for "Indian" comes to prevail.

The revelation of the past of the Milroy children comes not through Sally's efforts alone but through the co-ordinated confessions and unveilings of those who were of consequence to the family. There are four autobiographies that constitute the structural framework of *My Place*, namely, those of Sally Morgan, Arthur Corunna, Gladys Corunna and Daisy Corunna. Sally's quest for the truth about her family history and her urge to establish her identity as an Aboriginal is what links these four autobiographies. These four autobiographies, converging at critical points in the authors' lives, enable one to assess the events and characters from varied viewpoints and provide a means of corroborating and verifying facts that are reported by them: for example, a clearer picture of Bill Milroy's associate, Frank Potter, emerges after reading the accounts of both Sally and her mother, Gladys. Also, when Sally and her mother reach the homestead at Corunna Downs station they are happy to be able to identify the main house which conformed to the descriptions of Arthur and Nan: "It was concrete evidence that what Arthur had told us and what Nan had mentioned were all true." (290)

The stories are interwoven in more evident ways. Arthur's story inspires Sally to return to Corunna Downs so that his narrative determines the latter's subsequent reporting. Daisy's narrative, honestly communicated before her life comes to an end, enables Sally to conclude her labour with an affirmation of her grandmother's life and her own Aboriginal antecedents.

One focal point at which the four autobiographies comprising the narrative intersect is that which compels each one of the authors to render a sensitive account of the inhuman manner in which the Aboriginals were treated in Australia. The chief characters in this text, Gladys (Mum) and Daisy (Nan) construe their lives in terms of the Aboriginal female subordinated to the superior White male colonizer. They narrate the exploitation and oppression they had suffered due to the colonial ideological indoctrination and cultural subjugation. For them the past represents pain and humiliation caused by the White man, who had forcibly snatched them away from their homes and placed them in missions and settlements where they had been made conscious of their "shameful" heritage. Sally's regret, "Why was I cursed with being a girl?" (35), though expressed in a different context, has far-reaching implications.

Nan's outburst over her colouring, "You bloody kids don't want me, you want a bloody White grandmother, I'm black. Do you hear, black, black, black," and Jill's subsequent eruption, "Boongs, we're boongs! . . . A boong. You know, Aboriginal" change the meaning of life for Sally. It puts an entirely different perspective on her view of the past and as she herself proclaims, it "heralded a new phase in my relationship with my mother." (122) She has no qualms of conscience in declaring, "We had suddenly switched our allegiance from India to Aboriginal Australia." (176) With this sense of fidelity firmly entrenched in Sally's psyche she shot out a volley of questions at herself compelling her to adopt an introspective stance regarding her heritage:

> Had I been dishonest with myself? What did it really mean to be Aboriginal? I'd never lived off the land and been a hunter and a gatherer. I'd never participated in corroborees or heard stories of the Dreamtime. I hardly knew any Aboriginal people. What did it mean for someone like me? (179)

This regret at the lack of participation in the corporate life of the Aboriginals gives Sally a sense of guilt which makes her want to be able to say heartily with Arthur, "I'm proud of being a blackfella." (187) She tries to understand Nan's being ashamed of her past when Arthur explains the cause of his sister's complexes. "Aah, she's bin with whitefellas too long. They make her feel 'shamed, that's what White people do to you. Why should we be 'shamed, we bin here longer than them." (189)

It is in these words of Arthur that we register a sense of resistance defying the unwritten law of superiority that the Whites quote to subjugate the Black Aboriginals of Western Australia. Sally, too, having delved deep into the recesses of Western Australian history takes umbrage at the way her people were treated: "Aborigines were considered subnormal and not capable of being educated the way Whites were." (193)

Fear of discrimination against Aborigines had persisted in Nan for a long, long time, almost till the end of her life. She kept saying things like "Terrible things will happen to you if you tell people what you are." (350) and "There are still times when I'm scared inside, scared to say who I really am." (382) But then it is,

Sally who is largely responsible for the emergence of her grandmother and mother from the morass of fear and insecurity. She helps them confront the fact that they are Aborigines and persuades them to write their life histories, keeping nothing back from the present generation. Their narratives prove to be a cathartic experience that finally leads them to come to terms with their personal history. It is a traumatic ordeal but it helps them tide over the worst and gradually overcome the misery and sense of shame at having been a dispossessed and enslaved people. Once this feeling of humiliation is exorcized, Nan and Gladys, Sally's mother, start asserting themselves and their assertions verge on the rebellious. In an unmistakable tone of protest, Nan tells us:

> 'Cause you're black, they treat you like dirt. You see, in those days, we was owned, like a cow or a horse. I even heard some people say we not the same as Whites. That's not true, we all God's children. (419)

And again,

> I'm 'shamed of myself, now. I feel 'shamed for some of the things I done. I wanted to be White, you see . . . . Fancy, me thinkin' that. What was wrong with my own people? (419)

This sense of self-esteem, as it germinates in Nan's mind, brings with it a sense of identity and security, a consciousness of "belonging" somewhere. She could now very well say with Billy back home, "I belong here. It's good to be with my people." (296) Sally, too, after her rewarding visit to Corunna Downs station, triumphantly declares, "We'd seen so much of her and ourselves in the people we'd met. We belonged, now. We wanted her to belong too." (296)

An observation made by Jean Starobinski with regard to autobiography as a form of writing is fully applicable to Sally

Morgan's work: "The narrator describes not only what happened to him at a different time in his life but above all how he became . . . out of what he was . . . what he presently is."[13]

The entire meaning of life for Sally takes on a different colour after she discovers her Aboriginal origin. Clearly, the genesis of her present state of euphoria lies in her fruitful exploration of the past. It is this deep interest in the family history that also makes her conscious of the element of spiritualism that prevails in the Aboriginal culture. Aboriginal music, she was told, was heathen music and it often emanated from an unknown and undetected source. Nan, when she heard music coming from an unidentified origin had to be pacified by being told, "There's no one down there, it's a spiritual thing." (367) She herself, however, had firm faith in the spiritualism of the aborigines: "Blackfella know all 'bout spirits. We brought up with them. That's where the White man's stupid. He only believes what he can see. He needs to get educated. He's only livin' half a life." (429)

This contempt for the Whites is again an indication of the growing antagonism against them. The initial acceptance of their superiority now becomes a statement of their inferiority in spiritual matters. The Aboriginal bird, "something spiritual," (442) is beyond the comprehension of the Whites.

Interestingly, the title of the text, *My Place*, radiates a world of meaning. In the light of this title, the past events in the life of the author which were probably without much significance at the time of occurrence, acquire a new meaning. It is to this new meaning that the choice of incidents and details of her past life is geared. The term, "My Place," may refer to the physical location of a person, it may be an indication of one's social position, or, it may even have a spiritual connotation implying one's place in "the scheme of things" in the particular context of God's creations. For the Aborigines, their "place" may be their traditional land, and, in their culture, the physical and the spiritual are interlinked. "My Place," at various levels of meaning, covers all these concepts of "place" and the narrative concludes with an affirmation of Daisy's life and her Aboriginality. Running parallel to this is Sally Morgan's own assertion of her Native origin—for her it is a journey of the discovery of a rich Aboriginal heritage.

Morgan's epigraph to her book is meaningfully dedicated to "My Family" for it is a declaration of the invulnerable identity and integrity of a whole community that discovers itself afresh:

> How deprived we would have been
> if we had been willing
> to let things stay as they were.
> We would have survived,
> but not as a whole people.
> We would never have known our place. (296)[14]

Sally, after her visit to Corunna Downs station with her mother, ecstatically announces that there she felt "like we'd suddenly come home and now we were leaving again. But we had a sense of place now." (291) Sally's mother, proud to be an Aboriginal now, wants her children to identify with their past and to admit their Aboriginal origin, not conceal it as a matter of shame. She hopes that her children "will feel proud of the spiritual background from which they've sprung. . . . All I want my children to do is to pass on their Aboriginal heritage." (382) This hope of Sally's mother is not belied, for her daughter makes a virtue of her cultural Aboriginal heritage in embracing her spiritual and racial roots fondly and unashamedly.

NOTES

1. Arnold Oganov, "Art as a Form of Self-Awareness," Probl*ems of Contemporary Aesthetics*, compiled T. Lyubimova A. Zis and M. Ovsyannikov (Moscow: Raduga Publishers, 1984), p. 240.

2. Vassily Novikov, *Artistic Truth and Dialectics of Creative Work*, Eng. Trans. (Moscow: Progress Publishers, 1981), p. 14.
3. *Ibid.*
4. Rodney Hall, "Introduction," *Collins Book of Australian Poetry*, qtd. *Let Me Say*, Ramesh Mohan (Meerut: Shalabh, 1996), p. 105.
5. Pushpinder Syal, *Structure and Style in Commonwealth Literature* (New Delhi: Vikas, 1994), p. 4.
6. C.D. Narasimhaiah, "Australia: A Visitor's Impressions of the Land, Life and Literature," *Essays in Commonwealth Literature* (Delhi: Pencraft International, 1995), p. 173.
7. Cited in Ramesh Mohan, *Let me Say*, p. 108.
8. Alexei N. Tolstoy, *Collected Works*, Vol. 13, p. 352 (in Russian)
9. Victoria Laurie, "An Interview with Sally Morgan," *Southerly*, 23, No. 1 (999), p. 38.
10. Ronald Berndt, "Opening Address," *Aboriginal Writing Today*, p. 9.
11. James Olney, ed., "On Writing Autobiography," *Studies in Autobiography* (New York: O.U.P., 1988).
12. Sally Morgan, *My Place* (Fremantle, Western Australia; Fremantle Arts Centre Press, 1987), p. 123.
13. Jean Starobinski, "The Style of Autobiography," *Autobiography: Essays Theoretical and Critical*, ed. James Olney, p. 49.
14. These lines constitute the Epigraph to the book.

Sally Morgan's *My Place*: A Study

MEENAKSHI PAWHA
University of Lucknow

My Place begins as a warm, conventional account of Sally's early childhood years. The art of narrative is unique: it begins as an autobiographical account but has the stories of her great uncle, mother and grandmother succinctly woven into the matrix of the story.

The first half of Sally's narrative unravels the child's point of view. The initial chapter begins with her being "five year old in an alien environment." The frequent visits to the hospital are abominable to her. It is at the very outset that she introduces us to her father Bill Milroy, who ostensibly had been a prisoner of war. She shared an inexplicable bonding with him despite the household being dominated by alcoholism. There is adequate exemplification of their poverty when she narrates how she "burrowed deeper under the mound of coats and blankets piled on top of me," and "they were heavy and lacking in warmth" (13) and how she "shared a bed with my brother Billy and my sister Jill," who never felt the cold.

Sally's experience of schooling is rather unhappy. Chapter Two is entitled "The Factory"--quite symbolic of her experiences at school. She makes certain sociological comments: "When you turn six, you have to go to school, that's the law." Her reluctance and her mother's persuasion, vividly unfold the narrative and bring to us a world alive from the perspective of a little girl. The entire description about her staying back after the bell rang is reminiscent of many such instances of first-dayers at school. Sally has brought it alive in front of us. We are part of her world. Like any child of her age, she feels highly insecure and as she unravels her childhood the reader is made aware of the negative manner in which the school has impacted her life.

Sally remains ignorant of her background, carrying on with her life-oblivious of the fact that she is an Aboriginal. It is at school that she becomes aware of her different background. In the third chapter which is titled "I'm in the Army Now," she recalls her days in school, the tyranny unleashed by the peer group and how this had impacted her psyche, which have been very deftly handled by Morgan. The entire episode of a classmate drawing the attention of the whole class to her 'wetting herself' in the class has been very sensitively handled. It brings forth the pain, the trauma, the humiliation and the feeling of alienation that Morgan felt as a little girl. To add insult to injury was an equally insensitive, uncaring school teacher, Miss Roberts, who singled her out in the class. The helplessness that Morgan felt in combating such an embarrassing situation is very poignantly brought out in the narrative: "'Oh, there you, dear.' I had been cowering behind the girl in front of me, with my hands stuffed between my legs in an attempt to prevent further trickles" (25) "Grasping me by the elbow, she hauled me back to my desk and pointing to the offending puddle, demanded, 'And where have all those handkerchiefs come from? . . . I felt so embarrassed'" (26). Morgan is sent out of the class to "dry off" and her attitude towards the school took "an even more rapid downhill turn after that incident." She felt very alienated from the rest of her classmates whom she calls the "spick-and-span brigade," and herself, "the grubby offender."

The fourth chapter "Drinking Men" shows Bill Morgan's father who has a proclivity for drinks, and how "father's brothers were great drinkers too," and not one of his mates was a teetotaler (28). In fact Morgan attributes her "keen interest in drinking and smoking at a young age" to this environment at home and she became "adept at rolling Dad's cigarettes." The readers come to know that he has been a prisoner of war and that "Dad was the kind of man who enjoyed defying the odds. I think it gave him a sense of power he didn't normally have."

Chapter Five "Pretending" unravels the young Morgan's attempts at malingering to keep her away from the trauma of going to school, and now Nan, Morgan's grandmother would allow Billy, her younger brother, to stay back from school and "supported him in his dislike of school." This chapter is replete with humour, particularly the incident which Morgan narrates when she made pathetic attempts to stay back from school. Morgan tells the story in the most natural manner that the readers are made aware of a world which gives adequate glimpses into child psychology. She becomes aware of the social discrepancies between her classmates and herself because of her Aboriginal background. It is at this juncture of the narrative that Morgan unravels the question of identity—a question which has been immensely difficult for the Aborigine to answer. Her family is the epicentre. Responding to one of the kids, who made a remark about Morgan sharing a bed with her brother and sister, she told them: "We'd squeezed five in that bed." This emanates from the cultural differences between the Whites and the Aborigines. In fact Morgan "considered them disadvantaged." She couldn't explain "the happy feeling of warm security" she felt when they all "snuggled in together."

It is at school that children begin to question about her identity. They wanted to know which country Morgan came from. It is to this that her Mum told them to say that they were Indians—thus pretending to be someone other than themselves.

Chapters 6-10 succinctly describe the increased inebriation of Bill Milroy, his death, and the children's incapability of dealing with death. "'What are we s'posed to do?' . . . 'I s'pose we'd better cry,' and the questioning 'Sally . . . do ya think . . . we could . . . go outside and play now?'" Morgan was barely nine when she lost her father and the younger Helen "was only eighteen months old" (53). Throughout the narrative one thing is reiterated by Morgan and that is the need for family tries "about families sticking together (50). Mother managed to obtain war pension and it was "regular money" at a time when they needed it most. Morgan sees her mother getting empowered gradually by taking driving lessons, and although "she wasn't afraid to work," and had kept some money coming all those years when Dad was frequently in the hospital, "she increased her load and took on whatever jobs were going."

The influence of Nan on Morgan's life has been clearly brought out. Her enthusiasm for wild life and Nan being such an industrious worker, were all the things that impacted Morgan's life as a child. "Nan would never forgive us if she thought we'd been deliberately unkind to wild creatures." (56)

We get to know of the physical disability of Morgan after she contracted rheumatic fever. Amidst all that pain, she learnt a valuable lesson from "being that sick," she was "strong inside" (64). As she grows older, she begins to empathise with her Mum, when she realizes: "The time Mum spent in the toilet was her only chance for peace and quiet with five children in the house, where else could she go?" Nan's influence extended beyond her enthusiasm for the wild. It was "Nan who first brought out the skeptic" in Morgan. She infused suspicion about outsiders which extended to doctors as well.

Chapter 11-16 deal with Morgan's schooling phase. One significant incident that she narrates is of her mum being offered a job as a cleaner at her school, and how she had asked all the children whether it met their approval. Morgan failed to comprehend the ramifications of such a remark, as she was too naive to realize that being "a school cleaner carried with it very little status" (65) Morgan in grade six, celebration of Guy Fawkes night, the advent of David into school, Morgan's award at school are all vignettes of her school life. Her choosing a fairy tale book for her prize did not meet the approval of the headmaster, Mr. Buddee, but Morgan stuck to her choice as she knew that "fairy tales were the stuff dreams were made of." This is reminiscent of her Aboriginal roots of dreamtime.

The growing up period, an attempt of child sexual abuse by an uncle, are all deftly woven into the leit-motif of the novel (82). Morgan soon realized the social stigma that was attached to being Aborigine, and the innumerable stereotypes that shroud other people's judgments.

"She reckons all Abos are a bad influence" (98). Morgan realized that the only way to successfully survive in a White world was to assimilate and assimilation meant repudiating their past, their culture and even their family. And the final question about their identity. "What people are we?" (105) She had come to accept that Nan was dark and that their heritage was not shared by other Australians, yet she found it difficult to accept that they were Aboriginal.

Chapters 17-26 encapsulate Gladys (Mum) becoming a successful business woman and Morgan's sporadic attempts at study. Till then, she hadn't cared whether she passed on failed. But suddenly, Morgan began to make "earnest attempts at study" (109) and the very obvious contrast between her sister Jill and brother, Bill.

Morgan managed to secure a job as a clerk in the government department and this lasted about six months (113). After a consistent dislike for school, Morgan found the university to her liking (124). She enjoyed the freedom that is part of a university culture: "there were hours in the coffee shop, discussing the meaning of life." She met Paul, a school teacher, whom Morgan subsequently decided to get married, and moved to South Perth.

As Morgan settled to married life, the question of identity and a sense of belonging repeatedly crossed her mind, and the subject of Nan's origins always came up (134). After years of 'pretending' to be Indians, having denied their identity, lest their children be taken away, as the law entailed, Gladys confessed to being Aboriginal. "We're Aboriginal, aren't we, Mum?" "Yes dear" (135).

It is from this point that the story takes a different turn. Morgan is very excited by her "new heritage" (136) "and desperately wanted to do something" to identify her new-found heritage" (137). A gradual change takes place in Nan. She begins to get involved with the Aboriginal people and the oppression that they had come to face because of their colour.

Morgan shares her very intimate experiences of racism when she is harassed by the government machinery to prove her credentials as the authorities felt that her Aboriginal scholarship was under false pretensions. She realized it "hadn't been easy trying to identify with being Aboriginal." "No one was sympathetic, so many people equated it with dollars and cents, and no one understood why it was so important" (141). But she chose to stay on the scholarship, for denial of that would mean "denial of her tentative identification with the past (141).

Morgan graduated from the university and also gave birth to a daughter (145). It is around this time that her Nan's brother, Arthur, began making regular visits. When Arthur was around Nan was 'like a child' (147). It is at this juncture that Morgan saw Nan and Arthur "jabbering away in what sounded like a foreign language" (149), and the enormity of the fact that it must have been years since she used her own language (149). This propels Morgan to resolve to write a book. (150)

This resolve leads to another unravelling—the story of the Aboriginal past—they were considered "sub normal," "not capable of being educated the way Whites were" (151). The Herculean task that Morgan was saddled with was to persuade Gladys and Nan to speak who wanted to "leave the past buried" as "it won't hurt anyone" (152). But Morgan was determined to know her own history. Nan too puts up a lot of resistance in talking of her past and is incensed at Morgan's notion of writing a book. Gladys tries to convince her about Morgan's commitment to writing a book, as "there's nothing about Aboriginal people and what they've been through." (161) Her tenacity was rewarded when she meets the ninety-three year old Alice Drake-Brockman in a nursing home. It is from this narrative that we get the "links with the past"; how Gladys went to Parkville, and how different Australian society was in those days—with a strong English tradition amongst the upper classes.

From this point, Chapters 27-29, the autobiographical narrative is subsumed by Arthur Corunna's story. Here Morgan makes a very deft use of her artistic capability and this dovetailing of the narratives of Arthur, Daisy and Gladys, along with the story of her childhood and youth—Morgan has achieved a keen socio-cultural insight into the history of the Aborigines which till then had always been documented from the perspective of the White man. It was they who tempered history to suit their interpretation. Arthur Corunna's narrative transports us to the world of Arthur Corunna, of his being subjected to physical violence till "We bled" (186), and how he left the mission and was subjugated and exploited. (197) Eventually, Arthur's hardships come to a fruitful end when he bought a little farm in Mukinbudin. Being industrious, he soon rose to prominence, being the only farmer in the area to have a cheque book (199). He reiterated his concern for the Aborigines. He feels that colonialism is not over yet (212).

Further Gladys' narrative catapults us to the world of Aborigines with its distinct flavour of names, customs and traditions. The entire ethos is brought to life. Their life at Parkerville, of curfew being imposed which prevented Aboriginal people traveling after dark. (250) The loneliness that engulfed her life, as she had no family and deeply yearned to have one: "I often prayed to God to give me a family" (251), and her trips to Ivanhoe. The Depression of the 1930s made people so poor, especially Aboriginal people. She felt sorry for them as she "wondered how they could come to be so poor. They had nothing, especially the old ones. A lot of them had been separated from the young ones, all their kids had been taken off them, they had no one to look out for them." (262) Another poignant moment in Gladys' life was the incident of the "Black dolls." Alice places it in her arms and she cries out, "I don't want a Black doll," and Alice laughed. This entire episode is reminiscent of the bonded labour in the Indian context.

Moreover when Gladys turned fourteen she was worried that she'd be "sent out to work as a domestic" (270) and never see her mother again. Later on, she is unable to pursue her studies after school, and took up a job with a florist. (277) Subsequently, her marriage to Bill, despite strong opposition from the mother, clearly showed her determination to lead the rest of her life with him, though the marriage turned out to be a rather unhappy experience for Gladys. Bill's going to fight the war with children being born in quick succession—all led to Gladys' pain. Bill's prejudice is against being "just Aboriginals." He never liked "us having our people to the house" (300). With Bill's death, Gladys does feel a sense of "unburdening." There is a particular instance of the welfare lady visiting them and Gladys is mortified of the fact that she may find out that she is Aboriginal "and might have the children taken away." (304) What incessantly plagued her mind was that in a hundred years of time, there won't be any

Black Aboriginals left. "Our colour dies out; as we mix with other races" (306), a concern arising out of frequent miscegenation.

The last part of the book *My Place* ends with Daisy Corunna's story. At the age of fourteen, she was taken away from Corunna. Drake-Brockmans left others and took her in. Though she was Howden daughter, she did all the work at Ivanhoe. The cleaning, the washing, the ironing: "There wasn't anything she didn't do." Subjected to racial discrimination by the Whites, Daisy yearned that "God could make" her "White." (336)

The pain of separation from her daughter Gladys who was about three years old is poignantly brought out in the narrative (340). The re-appearance of her brother Arthur in Perth is yet another incident that is very moving in *My Place*. At fourteen, Gladys left Parkerville and Daisy wanted her to stay with her at Ivanhoe, but she was not allowed to stay there. A sense of rejection and betrayal is what Daisy felt, having been let down despite "promises," "the promises of wealthy family are worth nothing" (343). Daisy was most disheartened by the sudden marriage of Gladys and Bill, for she was only twenty-one, and she didn't like Bill as "he was a drinker" (344). Daisy came to live at Mulberry Farm when Gladys got polio, at a time when she was expecting Billy, and "she was stuck in bed" (346). The suffering and pain that they were subjected to because of Bill's drinking and schizophrenia are brought out in the narrative. This piecing of narratives together has been very dexterously achieved by Morgan. The problems faced by the family due to miscegenation were yet another serious matter of concern for Daisy. She feared: "they did not like people like us rearin' kids with White blood in them," and was paranoid that they may not "take Sally away from her" (348). She is concerned with the word, "Land Rights" and wonders whether they'll "give the Black fellas land" (349). In the last chapter "The Bird Call," Morgan narrates Nan's ill-health and her last days, as she lay in bed, dying of a terminal disease. She confessed to Sally. "Sal, . . . all my life, I been treated rotten, real rotten. Nobody's cared if I've looked pretty. I been treated like a beast." (352) This is an abysmally moving tale of an old woman whose life was reduced to something similar to the life of a beast of burden. The premonition that Nan has about her going away, "it was the Aboriginal bird Sally. God sent him to tell me I'm going home soon" (357) and "heard the bird call."

By weaving the narratives of Arthur Corunna, Gladys Corunna and Daisy Corunna's story, Morgan has, in *My Place*, reinscribed their oral accounts, not in sterile standard English, but according to their speech pattern i.e. the spoken Aboriginal English and she is surprised on hearing her grandmother speak. (351) Thus though the White form of expression is used, the narrative is closer to the Aboriginal literary tradition and by not tampering with the style Morgan retains the "Aboriginality." Thus Morgan makes a contribution to the evolving form and content and purposes of a vital and modern tradition of Aboriginal literature. She hasn't used the stream-of-consciousness technique but has unfolded the narrative in the most unusual way.

Structurally, the novel has a totally different form. Morgan could have begun by telling Nan's story, and Gladys and Arthur's—but she chooses to unravel their tales at the end of the novel dexterously juxtapositioning the western autobiographical form with the modern tradition of Aboriginal literature. How she achieves this unusual pastiche is worth looking into. *My Place* unravels itself with an account of Sally's early childhood years in a household dominated by the alcoholism and unpredictable behaviour of her father. Her mother Gladys and Grandmother, Nan (Daisy), combine to rear the children, attempting to disguise their Aboriginality by claiming to be of Indian origin. After Gladys's admission of their Aboriginal background, the nature of the book changes, the emphasis turning from Sally herself to the histories of her mother and grandmother. More information is disclosed when Sally's great-uncle Arthur (Daisy's brother) appears. Arthur and Daisy were born at Corunna Downs Station, near Marble Bar, owned by the Drake-Brockman family in the 1890s, the offspring of a full-blood Aboriginal woman and a White man. As all children of Aboriginal women and White men were taken away from the mother to be raised, Daisy later went to Perth as a servant in the Drake-Brockman household and her daughter Gladys to the Parkerville Children's Home. Uncompromising in her efforts to get at the truth of her background and to fully trace her family history, Sally and her mother travelled to the Corunna Downs area. Both Gladys and Nan felt compelled by that journey and its emotional impact to elaborate the painful history of all that had happened. From it all, Sally Morgan finally came to understand her place. The true importance of *My Place* is that it contains a story, the essence of which was repeated countless thousands of times in the early part of this century. Much more effectively and poignantly than a myriad historical studies and documentary accounts, the simple but anguished stories of Daisy, Arthur and Gladys Corunna have exposed the reality of White racism in Australia. It is humorous, sad, painful and deeply poignant.

"If there were a competition, Mum would be the best prayer in the neighbourhood" (64) or "I was merely suffering from growing pains. I had no idea that getting taller could be such agony" (64) or "we came to consider Nan's cigarettes as an extension of her anatomy" are few instances of the kind of humour that Morgan astutely punctuates her narrative with. The pain, the humiliation felt by Gladys when she was taken away to the Parkerville Children's Home, the incident of the Black-doll in the Drake-Brockman household, where their stay was synonymous with our own bonded labour. The fear of being found and the

Damocles' sword hanging perpetually over their heads added to an innate sense of insecurity which overwhelmed their minds. Morgan's compelling need to tell the tales for she feared that no one would ever know the deep-rooted discrimination felt by these Aboriginals, at the hands of White masters, the problems of miscegenation that arose out of such unions, are what punctuate the narrative and Morgan tells the tale with a lot of nerve and poignancy.

Sally Morgan's *My Place*: A Return from Exile

SANGEETA DAS
D.G. College, Kanpur

Reading through Sally Morgan's *My Place* fills me with appreciation for the author who has laid bare her own indigenous identity fighting through unfriendly circumstances and hurdles. She is not only hardworking but also brave as she was able to coax her reticent mother and grandmother into opening up their hearts and giving us a glimpse of the excruciating conditions under which they had led their lives and consequently had shrunk away from disclosing their identity. In order to have a respectable and safe life for themselves and their children, they went as far as disowning their nativity and culture. Both Gladys and Nan's autobiographies are heart-rending and spiritually torturous and anyone in their place would have done the same. Sally Morgan did a brave job in helping her mother and grandmother to accept their originality and also appreciate their nativity which happened to be the origin of Australia. Both Gladys and Nan used to shrink from the very idea of discussing their past as if it was so disgusting that its very thought evolved something painful which they wanted to keep in recess for good. Badly hit was Nan who had undergone a harrowing past being a complete blackfella.

The ill-treatment of a black skin by the White is not unknown. Everywhere the White have used Blacks according to their convenience and not refrained from discarding them when the need ended. Alice coaxed Nan by saying that they were one family but never was she allowed to forget that she was a servant and nothing else. Alice carefully separated Gladys from Nan when she was a mere three-year-old child on the pretext that she did not have enough money to feed her. Alice also laid restriction on Nan's visit to Gladys at Parkerville Children's Home. Imagine a child spending her childhood at a Children's Home when she had her mother to stay with. So much for Alice's assurance that they were one family.

On another occasion, Alice discharged Nan as she did not require her services anymore. Poor Nan was left high and dry when she luckily got a job with another family and that family gave her a rise in salary. Her brother Arthur had looked for a good White man who had agreed to marry Nan. When things were well set for Nan, Alice coaxed her back, reminding her about her good old days with her. Nan, in her sincerity towards Alice, left the job and her prosperous happy married life and joined in with Alice on the old pay scale. This shows that Nan was not ungrateful while Alice was a mean creature who emotionally exploited Nan emotionally and used her for her needs.

Nan was not much shocked by Alice's attitude because she was aware of the fact that the latter was a White and could never be one with her into a family. The Whites and their children had the privilege of growing up amidst their family and going to school while she and her children were destined to stay back at home and serve them as servants for the reason of being black.

The Blacks may be outwardly black and uncomely but inwardly they were also human beings of flesh and blood with feelings and emotions. They revolted sub-consciously but suffered quietly because they knew they could not defy the White who were more powerful than them and also comprised the government. However the 1960s and early 70s saw a change in attitude and White writers championed racial tolerance.

Simultaneously, a movement among the Natives tried to expose the injustices suffered by themselves at the hands of the White settlers and revive their almost vanished traditions and culture. Before the White came, the Aboriginals did not know how to write, so their literature was maintained orally and thus unknown to others. Later most of their literature was recorded in writing and many transcribed their past. As aptly conveyed by Morgan:

> there's almost nothing written from a personal point of view about aboriginal people. All our history is about the white man. No one knows what it was like for us. A lot of our history has been lost, people have been too frightened to say anything. . . . There are, all sorts of files about aboriginals that go way back and the government won't release them. . . . And they don't like letting them out because there are so many instances of police abusing their power when they were supposed to be protectors of aborigines that it's not funny! I mean our own government had terrible policies for aboriginal people. Thousands of families in Australia were destroyed by the government policy of taking children away. None of that happened to white people. (161)

Gradually, the assertion of an identity in their own motherland came alive and through the capacity to write, the atrocities incurred by the natives at the hands of the White settlers came to light. Sally Morgan, the author, a daughter of a half-Aboriginal mother and a White father, remained ignorant about her aboriginal past till she was fifteen and was enlightened by her younger sister, Jill that they were of Aboriginal descent. She wanted to confirm this from her mother and grandmother who vehemently denied their aboriginal ancestry and would not talk about the past. Though Sally knew that the denial was deliberate, she was in the dark about the cause and this puzzled her deeply and strengthened her curiosity. She finally was determined to unravel the mystery of their origin and this resulted in *My Place* which not only threw light on her past but justified her mother and grandmother's fears of being known as natives and ostracized and the progress of their children stunted.

In *My Place*, we come across three generations—Nan, Gladys and Sally. Nan being a complete Aboriginal, was the worst sufferer of all. She had a very harsh life of suffering, torture and servitude and only when her daughter Gladys started working after Bill's death did she have enough to eat. Throughout her life in the past, she could not recollect a day when she had a proper lunch or was not hungry. She saw the White's overfed and eat in expensive crockery and desired only to possess a cup and a saucer. Therefore when her grand-daughters grew up and asked her what she wanted as a gift, she said a cup and a saucer. She could also not forget the piercing glare of the White s because she was a black. She was denied good food, good clothes and a proper roof over herself. There was practically nothing which Nan could call hers. She was supposed to be submissive as a Black and had no say before a White. The White treated the Black as dirt. Owning them was just like one who would own an animal and make it work hard and any deterrence would be curbed by flogging. Daisy (Nan) had heard people say that Whites and Blacks were different and the Blacks were nothing in comparison to the Whites while she knew well at heart that it was not true as they were all God's children.

The mental pressure and disgrace was predominant during her time so much so that at a stage, Daisy fancied herself as White and prayed to God for a transformation from Black to White. She thought that was the best God could do for her. Such was the impact of White over the Black. It took years of mind-wrestling and the boldness of her grandchildren to come out with her secrets in Sally's book and make her feel ashamed of fancying herself to be White. Nan was an imposing figure throughout the text and a strength to Gladys through the problem years with

Bill. In this matriarchal family, she was the eldest and constant in her thoughts and belief. Fancy Daisy (Nan) questioning herself: "What was wrong with my own people?" It was the native who did the actual bit of work. They did the building and all sorts of hard labour. The Whites never did any type of hazardous work. Even the station where Nan passed the major part of her life was built by the natives. If it wasn't for the natives, nothing would get done. Therefore the White settlers did not allow them to have families. They feared that clustering as families they would grow stronger and could rise up against them. To curb any such possibilities, they snatched away their children from them and deposited them in homes saying that they were taken away from them for education. They were shifted from homes to various houses where they were made to work like servants. The children craved to be near their parents like Gladys whose adolescent-stage passed craving for her mother's company. Her mother also did not show much eagerness to keep her to herself for the fear of losing her forever. This trick was used by the Whites to break the Blacks emotionally and spiritually. The children pined for their parents and slogged quietly feeling at a loss and broken while the parents kept thinking about their little ones away from them and had no time to think about their own sufferings and rise in revolt against the Whites.

The White settlers were dishonest people as well. They bluffed the ignorant Blacks continuously. Their children were taken away from them on the pretext of getting them educated when no such thing happened. The parents and the children could not communicate as both did not know how to read and write. Nan was taken away from her mother for being educated while she was installed in the White's house as a servant. She felt helpless as she couldn't write to her poor mother about the actual condition due to her being illiterate.

Nevertheless, the Black woman who worked in houses of the Whites was not safe. There were many native women who had children from White men, not because they wished but because they were forced into it. It was a pitiable condition in which the native women led their lives. Being treated so brutally in one's own homeland, Nan could also have fallen prey to such circumstances when Arthur her elder brother popped into the picture. Both were thrilled to meet each other. He also had been snatched away from their mother when he was small. Her brother's support was a great help for Nan in the world of strangers where she was absolutely alone.

The Blacks were employed by the Whites and made to slog hard in their gardens and houses but were never paid any wages. Daisy (Nan) never saw a penny trickle down from Alice's pocket though she had been working there since she was a child. Rather she was kicked out at will and coaxed back and then kicked out again. In spite of hard and long labour, Daisy (Nan) could not afford to even visit her only daughter who had been snatched away from her.

Though Daisy (Nan) had suffered limitlessly and silently, she herself could not see people suffering from hunger whether White or Black because she believed it was not the blackfella's way. Starkly in contrast to this, the Whites who were plentifully blessed still craved for more and snatched away from the Blacks what little they had with them and left them stranded in their own homeland.

Blacks were deprived of the rights to the land in their own country whereas the White men had land rights for years. Arthur, a strong and hardworking Black, had the capacity and labour to turn a barren land into a fertile land and therefore flourished but his success was intolerable to the Whites and they put hurdles in his way and made his life difficult.

The Whites left no stone unturned to make the lives of the Blacks miserable and distressing. This suppression made the Black ashamed of their own heritage and they tried to hide their own originality. Nan and Gladys taught their children to call themselves Indians if they were asked about their identity. Jill's words, "It's a terrible thing to be Aboriginal. Nobody wants to know you. . . . You can be Indian, Dutch, Italian, anything but not Aboriginal" indicated the prevalent discrimination against the Aboriginals.

In the school, the White children were expected to show better results than the Blacks. They were given better opportunities and moreover when caught in mischief, were told to show better attitude than the Aborigines because they were better than the Aborigines in every aspect. The aborigines were not allowed to prosper or possess anything, not even their own children, and they remained in the quagmire of paucity.

Gladys could not study further because of poverty, but desired her children to acquire maximum education for which she sloggedday and night.

The Blacks were subjugated by the White settlers in every way. The Blacks were never expected to step ahead in any field be it family or education. Arthur's ownership of land was greatly disliked by the Whites for the Blacks were sought to work in the fields owned by the Whites. The Blacks had to wait upon the Whites and remain at their beck and call. They had bells which they rang whenever they needed something and the Blacks had to run to his service. Nan also disliked this bell business: 'Why do White people like ringing bells so much?'

The White had lots of food stowed away in the pantry which Nan and her friend stole and ate during siesta time for they were hungry. The Blacks were denied proper food by the Whites though they worked hard for them. In Nan's narration, she has stressed from time to time, that Blackfellas may be deprived, poor and illiterate but they were not inhuman like the Whites. They wouldn't let a dog go without his tea.

Revolt against the atrocities of the White was sizzling in the hearts of the Blacks. Though they did not have the courage and resources to voice their anger, the children tried to oppose them and thought it a brave deed.

Hunger can drive man to do anything. However a child can find it real difficult to resist itself when constantly under its impact. Daisy never had her stomach full and no wonder got into trouble over food. In one incident, she had to carry a pie from Nell to Mrs. Stone, she couldn't resist the appetizing smell of the pie and so had a dig. Daisy then squashed the pie and tried to make it look as before. She had to hand a note over to Mrs. Stone along with the pie. Poor girl could not read or write so did not know that Nell has directed Mrs. Stone in that letter to send the note back if she suspected tampering with the pie. Mrs. Stone handed back the note to be given to Nell who gave Daisy a nice whipping with the bullock canes. This was another reason for keeping the Blacks illiterate so that they remain ignorant to the machinations of the Whites.

It being a White's world, any association with them was considered a privilege. But the children from the White men were not allowed to stay with Black mothers. Only the Black ones could be retained by them. The White children were taken away if the Black mothers were considered incapable of raising them properly.

This was atrocious. The Blacks were hit emotionally and thus felt very low. The wedge between the Whites and the Blacks was so sharp that the native girls would not look at a Black fella. Daisy found herself stuck half way as she was too Black for the Whites and too White for the Blacks.

It was considered a big thing if a Black girl could marry a White man. Quite a number of natives who were lighter in colour, cleverly passed themselves off as White. One can only pity such people and not condemn them since the life of a native was so hard. The White on the other hand married a native on the condition of her severing every tie from the natives. Daisy's friend married a Slav. She came to say good bye to her and Nellie. She had promised her husband never to talk or mix with natives again. They all cried together. Daisy had no complaints against her. The Slav wouldn't have married her otherwise.

Being Black was like a stigma and a matter of constant shame. Daisy had to face many embarrassing situations, just because she was black. For instance, the minister at Christ Church had started up a sewing circle for all the native servants. One day, when Daisy was sitting with others sewing, the boys from Christ Church Grammar School passed that way. They laughed at them and called them awful names. They even went so far as to throw pebbles at them just as one would do with street dogs. Daisy was so ashamed that she never went there again.

During the days of shame and disillusion, Arthur came around as a real support and pleasant change for Daisy. His arrival gave Daisy a reason to look forward to the moments when they could be together. Both of them had met after ages. When Arthur was snatched away from his mother, Daisy was a small child and did not know much about Arthur except that he was her brother.

Daisy had a baby before she gave birth to Gladys. That baby was taken away from her. Obviously it must have belonged to some White fella. She did not disclose the matter to Gladys. Howden was Gladys's father but never married Daisy. His fatherly feeling surfaced when he realized that he may not survive. He said, 'Bring her here, let me hold her.' He wanted to nurse Gladys, before he died. After he died, Gladys was taken from Daisy as suspected at an age of three and sent to Parkerville for education. Daisy found the place wasn't bad when she visited it.

Gladys had many kids to play with which was a reason for relief to Daisy.

The Black servants had in a way mortgaged their life and future to the Whites. They had no say in the decisions concerning their life. Little Gladys no doubt had small friends at Parkerville to play with, nonetheless she wanted to stay close to her mother which Daisy knew but what could she do? 'It wasn't like I had a place of my own. It wasn't like I had any say over my own life.'

When Gladys was fourteen and had to return to Parkerville after spending her holidays with Daisy at Ivanhoe, she did not wish to stay there and so Daisy brought her back with her to Ivanhoe where she met with an opposition from Alice. Daisy had to make supplementary arrangement for Gladys to stay with another family. But the Hewitts after sometime refused to keep Gladys with them for she was a bad influence to other kids as she watched movies which was a sin.

Finally Gladys came to stay with Daisy who had been kicked out by Alice from Ivanhoe for the second time and was staying on her own. Alice owed her back wages which were never given. All these years Alice made her work for nothing and then kicked her out at will. Whenever she paid her some amount, Alice took it back by saying that Daisy owed her that. It had really been a hard life for Daisy. But being a Black, she dared not raise her voice.

The Whites led a lavish life and thus squandered their money on pomp and show. Daisy never saw any of their money. Howden had promised in his life-time to leave back some money for Daisy and Arthur but did not do so. This filled Daisy with more bitterness for the Whites. She considered them rotten and greedy. While leaving, Daisy got a couple of odds and ends and an old broom from Alice. After all the years of sincere service, this was all Alice could give her. Daisy came to know later that when an old servant left job, she would get a gold watch. Let alone the watch, Daisy had asked for a picture of Fremantle which she was denied as it was being sent to the auction house. There were other pictures which she had asked for, but they preferred to consign them to the fire than give it to the servant. So much of heartlessness in human-beings leaves us tearful. A servant, no matter to what colour or creed she or he belongs, is after all God's creation. How can a human-being show so much of indifference and viciousness to the other? Daisy spent the peak time of her life labouring in their household, suffering all humiliation and atrocities meted out to her, and was denied even the picture which was of no use to them.

Daisy was happy that blackfellas scored one above the Whites because they know all about spirits. They are brought up with them. It's here that the White man is ignorant. He only believes in what he can see. He is living only a partial life. The Blacks are no doubt adept at witchcraft. They use it to cure people. Daisy helped Gladys with polio when she was hit by it. Their family always had that power. Gladys was completely cured and could lead a normal life again.

Daisy's submissive and quiet nature came to light once again when she spoke about her life to Sally and said that her father, Bill, used to call her a bloody nigger when Gladys was not around. It had hurt her badly but she preferred to keep quiet. One particular quote sums up this aspect of hers. Sally writes: "I don't know why mum ever bothered to try to reason with her. After years of living with Nan, she should have realised that there did not necessarily have to be a direct connection between any two natural events for Nan to feel she was doing the right thing by protecting us from possible danger." (74)

Daisy's shunning government people had a reason behind it. She was constantly under the fear of losing her grandchildren because she knew they did not like people like them rearing kids with White blood in them. The fear was so predominant that

Daisy tried to stay out of the family after Bill's death because one look at her and one could tell she was a native. Gladys could have passed for anything. She told Gladys to make the children call themselves Indian if she wanted to save them from being taken away.

So much of suffering in Daisy's life did not change her nature; rather it filled her with great dislike and hatred for and fear of the White men. Not only did she shun her nativity but also made her daughter and grandchildren forget what they actually were. She says at one point to the kids, "you bloody kids don't want me, you want a bloody White grandmother, I am black. Do you hear, black, black, black!" (97) Years of suffering had made her stubborn and immune to the demanding changes of the time. Any reference to the inception of their clan would put her off.

Sally's constant coaxing, nudging and bullying to disclose her past so that she and her mother pick up the strings to their indignity made Daisy open up. The years had softened her outlook and helped her to disclose something from the past. But she felt less ashamed of being their grandmother and of being a member of the Black community as a whole. She also wanted her grandchildren to achieve success in life and not lead a stunted life like herself. With the utopian idea of the Blacks being treated like the Whites one day and allowed free mixing with them, she happily ends her story.

Though Sally could not get much out of her grandmother yet whatever she could, endeared her to the latter and this was no mean achievement towards her past.

Before Sally could get her grandmother to speak, she and her mum travelled to all those places which they thought were connected with Daisy's life and came to know quite a lot. The natives there were not only surprised to see them but also happy to know about Daisy's family because they all remembered her and Arthur.

Arthur on the other hand was never so much afraid of showing himself up as a Black. He adored the grandchildren and loved Gladys and came to visit them quite often. When he came to know about Sally's book to be written on the family history, he agreed to give his piece without disclosing much about Daisy's life which she herself would disclose if she wanted to do so. Nevertheless, Sally was quite excited by the opportunity he represented on her journey for her family identity.

The aboriginals were not allowed anything which the Whites desired to have. Once Arthur took a big, round and red tomato from a vegetable garden which was seen by Dudley, Howden Drake-Brockmen's brother who probably also had an eye on the tomato and labelling it as stealing, got Arthur lacerated by his own father. Arthur had no grudge against his father for he never hit Arthur unless on such occasions when he was forced to do so or he had to lose the job. Such was the viciousness of the Whites. Arthur was beaten up by Pixie, Dudley's son, while playing but he dared not touch him for fear of his father. His mother also cautioned him:

> Jilly-yung, never beat Pixie in a fight.
> When he wants to fight, you walk away.

As kids, Arthur had a good time with his brother Albert who was older to him. Later he was rounded up for education. He resisted it but how can a black's resistance work before White's persistence. He was forbidden to speak his blackfella's language. They had to speak English or Dudley beat him up.

Things were hard for the blackfellas in those days. Arthur often saw native people chained around the neck and hands walking meekly behind a policeman. The very sight brought tears in his eyes. Sometimes he heard that Whitemen went shooting blackfellas for sport just like animals. Such incidents filled Arthur's heart with fear. He did not wish to be treated so. Who would? Given the circumstances, his life would have been a great success. He had overcome much prejudice and had worked to own a farm.

Arthur being half blood was taken away from his mother. His brother Albert was also taken along with him. His sister Lily was left behind because she was full-blooded black. From their mother's lap, they were taken away and dumped in a mission where they were called inmates just as in a prison. Life there was also not peaceful. Arthur had to fight for himself and his brother Albert to make a place for themselves. When the mission was visited by the Englishman called Governor Bedford, the darker kids were separated from the lighter ones. He didn't like the lighter ones mingling with the darker ones.

Flogging of the black children was quite common during that time. Once when Arthur and a few other boys emerged out of the station and traced by Coulson, they were trooped back, and locked in on a roof-top and asked to strip off. After they were naked, Caulson chased them round and round the dormitory, wielding a long cane. He didn't care where he hit them with the cane. It came whacking on their head and body. The boys cried with pain and implored him to stop, calling him 'master' which he liked to hear. Arthur wouldn't call him 'master' or cry out which angered him all the more and he kept flogging Arthur till his thighs were running with blood. However, Arthur did not give him the pleasure of seeing him crying and pleading to him for mercy.

Though the Black workers worked harder and more hazardously, they were separated from the Whites even during lunch and dinner by sitting at different tables.

Arthur used to wonder why everyone liked an ugly bloke like him but I reckon it must have been because of Arthur's capacity to do hard labour. A hardworking Black was in demand everywhere. Despite his strength he had a keen sense of humour.

Sally writes: "Arthur was like mum, it wasn't often that he failed to see the funny side of things." (156) From 1913 to 1916, he had worked for Hancock. He was only given food but no pay though he was promised ten bob a week. He had no proper shelter for him and most of the time, he had to freeze in the cold. There was no proper place for him to sleep and in winter the icy cold wind slashed right through, making life hell for Arthur. He used to get old gallon tins and fill them with hot water, tie bags around them, then strap them to his feet. The tins gave some relief to his icy cold feet. He used to work real hard and most of his work was with his bare feet with which he used to tread the mud.

Arthur was never without work. He did not fear work and Whites always needed strong Blacks who could work hard and not hassle about money. It was through sheer hard labour that Arthur became the envy of all other farmers by possessing a cheque book out of which he paid the six men who worked for him. All the other farmers were mortgaged to the bank and naturally were jealous of him, a Black man doing better than them.

Howden had promised Daisy and Arthur some money after his death but what he bequeathed to Arthur was a pile of old photographs which he knew would not be claimed by anyone. Whites would not like to part with anything except trash for the Blacks.

Arthur was not only hardworking and sincere but also tender-hearted and honest. Girls chased him but he wouldn't go with any girl because he did not want them to get into trouble. This was evidence enough that Blacks were not bad and immoral as the Whites thought them to be. They also had morals and a heart full of emotions and fear for God.

Having imbibed a lot by his experiences, he ably articulated the plight of the aborigines and the pain that they had endured. He made very clear to Sally that he didn't want his story to be mixed with the White version of the family history. He proved to be an excellent story-teller and created a vivid picture of his times through his story.

A characteristic of the Whites stressed in *My Place* is their greedy nature. Daisy (Nan) reveals this in her narration and so does Arthur. Jack Edwards a White man already had other farms but wanted Arthur's which he had improved with his untiring labour. 'A White man gets greedy, he wants to take everything.'

The progress of a Black man was intolerable for a White man. Arthur's hard labour had enabled him to reach up to that stage when he could offer to buy a header. Buying the header was a thing out of the ordinary, to be a Black man and ahead of everybody else. Immediately he was falsely summoned by Wesfarmers and harassed by a policeman. He had to take the help of a lawyer to get out of this mesh. But it was the White's world and Arthur had to be pulled down to satiate their ego. Thus later during the Depression, he was summoned by the Agricultural Bank and to get by, he had to mortgage his farm, which was exactly what they wanted. At once they sold up everything, all his machinery except his horses. Now Arthur had nowhere to take his horses to without a farm. Finally, he had to sell them at a throwaway price, to be shot for pig feed. Arthur wonders: "Can you tell me that was fair, for all my pioneering days, to be treated like that?"

Blacks were meant to be servants serving the Whites and not to rub shoulders with them as equals. It was really hard for a Black man to get ahead. Struggle was his fate and Arthur had to struggle under all disabilities and hardship on his new land. Black war heroes were also not treated properly. They were denied citizenship and the right to vote. It was their own country but they were not free. The real blackfellas were in more trouble—the ones out of work and battling for a living. They worked for the farmers and paid back in kind. They cleared the land, put the crops and pulled sandalwood. The blackfellas even tracked the dingoes and hunted them down. Blackfellas did their share of tough work well in Mucka and made it what it is today.

For all the hard-work, Blacks always received suspicion and maltreatment from the Whites. While ending his story, Arthur was sad because he knew that colonialism had not ended yet. There was a White Australian policy against aborigines. Though it is said that they are all Australians and there is no difference between Black and White, it seems to be an eyewash and nothing else. The government has been robbing the Black man for years. The Whites did not want them to own land. The government itself may not have wanted that piece of land but would not allow the Blacks to own it. Why the Whites could not leave the Blacks alone? The Blacks had their rain song to bring rain for their lands and the warm weather to bring comfort in winter season. The Blacks killed the animals when they were hungry, not like the Whites who killed for sport.

Arthur's story moved Gladys into tears. She was happy to get something from the past to hang on to and be proud of. Such a brave uncle, who untiringly fought against the pernicious Whites and lived to be as old as ninety, was a person to reckon with.

Gladys's own life was not very peaceful and happy. As narrated by Nan, she was snatched away from her at the tender age of three or four. A baby at that stage wanted nothing more than a cuddle and kiss which she never got from the House Mothers who weren't like real mothers. The older aboriginal girls gave her a cuddle and kiss which filled her with a sense of security though they were not related to her. The older White girls looked down upon the Black kids and seemed not to care about anyone. Gladys had nightmares at night and craved for the warmth of her mother's body next to her but had to satisfy herself with the presence of God and gradually became attuned to spiritual influence and aboriginal music cuddling her to sleep.

Food there was equally bad. Gladys hated porridge as the weevils were there every morning staring out at her from her porridge bowl but could not forgo it as she was always too hungry to do so. Besides a slice of bread and dripping, porridge was all that she got for breakfast before leaving for school. During lunch, she got bad-smelling meat as hot as a stew. Tea was usually cold. However, the House Mother had butter on her toast and plenty of scalded cream. Mrs. Moore, the house mother, was a short-tempered lady and it did not pay to anger her. When angered, she inflicted terrible beatings. Inhuman labour and half-fed stomach was what the Black kids were bestowed with. Gladys was famished all the time, she ate the wild cranberries that grew in the bush and were sweet and juicy, and roasted potatoes which burnt her tongue. The best feed she had was gilgies. Such were the supplementary provisions which compensated for the lack of food from the house. Once separated from her mother, she belonged to the Native Welfare Department and was not even allowed to have the comfort of being with her own mother.

Things were real difficult for the Blacks. The White kids had all the facilities and comforts. But the aboriginal kids had a hard life. There was no one to see them and come to meet them. Their parents were hundreds of miles away and most of the time denied permit to travel. No one cared if they needed it to visit their children who were expecting their parents with tearful eyes.

Gladys's mother also had to face difficulties to come to meet her which Gladys realized when she grew up. There was a time when Nan did not visit Gladys for a long time and that made her anxious. Being an orphan was one thing but having a parent and still not being able to get her love was an excruciatingly painful experience.

The right place of a Black was the place of a servant at a White's house. A Black servant mother's daughter is also supposed to be a servant and nothing else. This statement was symbolically established in the incident when Gladys was presented by Alice with a Black topsy doll dressed like a servant. It had a red-check dress on and a White apron just like her mother. It also had a slave cap on its head as her mother wore on the washing days. The doll was a symbolic indication of the established slavery of the Blacks and mastery of the Whites. Gladys was absolutely stunned for she wanted to become a princess and not a servant.

The Blacks were the unruly clan in the eyes of the Whites. Whenever damage was done or if any argument arose between a White and a Black, obviously the Black had to supplicate. Everything went against the Black and he was never believed. Frustration reigned high amongst the Black especially the kids. In the Home where Gladys stayed, they were made to feel ashamed of being aboriginals.

Their life at home was like living amidst strangers etching out a place of their own by themselves. Small girls, when they grew up into young girls, needed the guidance of their mother to acquaint them with facts of life. They were totally unaware about the things which could happen to their bodies. The older girls who should have taken the place of mothers and taught them the reality, kept everything a secret and laughed amongst themselves. Under such circumstances, the ignorance could have made easy baits for mischief-mongers. There had been many cases of kids being molested but luckily, Gladys stayed out of it all. No one would believe a Black girl anyway even if she complained.

Gladys always nursed a dream of being a member of a big, happy family which she felt would be fulfilled when she went to stay with her mother at Ivanhoe but her dreams came crashing down like a house of cards when Alice refused to continue Gladys's stay at Ivanhoe and made it very clear that she was not wanted there.

Gladys was crestfallen when she was disowned by the owners of that place which was the only place which she thought was her home. But she dared not protest for she knew Aboriginal people like her weren't allowed to have families and it was because of this that she and her mum had to keep a low profile. The feeling of insecurity as an Aboriginal became pronounced when Gladys met a woman at the bus stop who was extremely grieved to know that she was an Aboriginal which shadowed her beauty. The lady's grief greatly moved Gladys and she experienced terrible dejection which changed into fright when her Mum told her not to reveal again before anyone, her nationality. The incident had cut a deep niche in Gladys's mind and she started wishing she was someone different. She became conscious of people staring at her mother whose aboriginality couldn't be hidden because of her broad features. The feeling was awful. It made her feel like an outcaste and a criminal. Suddenly Gladys's carefree world changed into an uncertain one where her future became a big question mark. Several questions arose in Gladys's mind which she wanted her mother to answer. But her mother would not disclose anything except 'Terrible things will happen to you if you tell people what you are.' This caution was enough to push Gladys into her shell as she was scared of authority and did not wish to create more difficulties in a life which she now knew was fraught with nothing less.

Later Gladys married Bill who had accepted her in spite of her being an aboriginal but neither Gladys's mother accepted Bill because of her suspicion about the Whites nor did Bill's parents accept Gladys because of her aboriginality. Their indifference towards the family continued even after the death of their son, when Gladys tried to maintain a relationship with Bill's parents. They rejected Gladys and her family because of their colour. Though Bill had married Gladys, inwardly he was never accommodating towards her about which Nan was very much aware. He never let go an opportunity of abusing her behind Gladys's back. To maintain peace in the family, Nan never revealed it to her daughter except when she related her story to Sally.

Bill was a heavy drinker and would not give it up though Gladys kept trying. His bouts were so deadly that he would get into murderous fits, for which reason Gladys had asked Nan to hide the axe. Bill was an utter failure as a husband. Instead of being a moral and financial support to the family, he was a constant drain on the purse. He had nightmares and the more he drank, the poorer the family became. Gladys had a tough time handling an alcoholic and sick husband and five children. No matter how much the other characters spoke well of him, Bill appears to have been a self-centred and heartless man who, instead of being polite to Gladys, was cruel towards her. Many people must have wondered why Gladys carried on with the persistent suffering inflicted on her by an incompatible husband and did not separate from him. Here her aboriginality shackled her feet tightly barring any possibility of escaping from her White husband. Bill had threatened her that if ever she decided to leave him, he would make sure that the kids were taken away from her. He said: 'Nobody will let someone like you bring up kids and you know it. I'm the one that'll get custody, I'll give them to my parents.'

Though Bill and Gladys had a love marriage and Bill had accepted her in spite of her aboriginality against the desires of his family and Gladys was ably putting up with his idiosyncrasies with patience and forbearance, the underlying current of difference between a White and an aborigine was not absent to the great disappointment of Gladys and Sally. The threat of losing her children from Bill was enough to make Gladys's heart sink and flushed out all the thoughts she had of separating herself from Bill. After Bill's death, there was every possibility of the children being snatched away from them as aboriginals were not allowed to raise children from a White father. It was then that Nan and Gladys both decided to hide their nationality from the children to save them from having a bad time. Moreover, too much of publicity might cause the welfare people to come and take away the kids which would kill both of them.

When Sally grew up and came to know about her nationality, she became curious rather than disgusted. She wanted to know more for which she wanted her mother and Grandmother to open up their hearts and let her into the past. An absolute contrast to Bill was Paul. He was a great emotional and moral support to Sally when often she broke down on her emotional trip back to her originality. Moreover, in his consideration for his wife, he placed his own needs second to his wife's. In a nutshell, Paul was a positive influence on Sally's journey to her inner self. Through their past, she would reveal to the world the atrocities done on the aborigines. Her enthusiasm filtered into her mother who felt awful that they had deprived the children of their heritage thinking they were doing the right thing. Gladys was embarrassed to think about everything she had said but she feels that 'Let me pass this way but once and do what good I can. I shall not pass this way again. Maybe someone else is walking a road that's like mine.'

Sally was remorseful while going through both Gladys's and Nan's story. Their innocence and suffering brought tears into her eyes. She felt her Grandmother's fear of the Whites was not unfounded altogether. Nan was recovering from her disillusionment when she underwent a harrowing experience in the hospital where she was manhandled by the doctors as an experimenting object. Her cry of pain fell on deaf ears. Sally was incensed over the whole incident but kept quiet for the benefit of her younger sister, Helen, who was gaining medical education.

Sally Morgan did not have any personal grudge against anyone but being a bright and optimistic young woman she felt it her duty to focus on the downtrodden but highlighting their sufferings and to appeal to the general public and the government to secure their rights.

In *My Place*, she starts with the experiences of her own life, revelation of her aboriginality, which forms the turning point in her life and motivates her to make her mother and grandmother unleash their tongues and unveil the past. In the process of gathering information for her book, she travels back to her grandmother's birthplace and comes to know about many incidents and meets many people which help her to make her book more effective. She starts the book with the aim of revealing her family history but it turns out to be an emotional and spiritual journey down the memory lane to the tentative past.

Her intention was to bring the Whites and the Blacks on an even ground as the aboriginals were the original inhabitants of the country. No wonder her autobiography *My Place* was the winner of the 1987 Australian Human Rights Award for Literature and subsequently the 1990 Order of Australia Book Prize.

Racism in the Aboriginal World of Sally Morgan's *My Place*

HARPREET KAUR

Panjab University, Chandigarh

My Place is Sally Morgan's journey into her past to expose the silence of the marginalised. The book is an autobiographical account of her childhood, schooling and journey from adolescence to marriage. Various incidents are described in detail to allow the reader an intimate feel of the life of the family. She travels backwards into history to expose the way her grandmother, mother and other Aboriginal relatives were treated by the Whites. She wants to announce to the White Australians the pain and sufferings of the Aboriginal people. When Morgan realizes that she is part Aboriginal, the search for her roots, her identity, here home begins: "the feeling that a very vital part of me was missing and that I'd never belong anywhere. Never resolve anything."[1] In her search for truth Morgan includes the autobiographies of her mother and grandmother, so that the various narratives reveal a complex network that the White imperialists had burdened the Aboriginals with. It is a significant milestone in Aboriginal literature as Morgan's self-discovery leads to confrontation with suppressed history, culture and community.

Morgan wants to get at the root cause of her grandmother's bitterness. She wonders what it felt like to be really dark-skinned with broad features. The White man's world treated the natives like dirt, whipped them to obey, pointing out to their lack of intelligence. The Government, too, would exact intensive labour from the Blacks but the harvest of gold was reaped by the mining companies. The Whites would refer to them as 'bloody mongrels' and sub-normals incapable of being educated. The industry was built on slave labour. If the Blacks refused to obey/work, the White man called in the White police. They would be chained around the neck and hands, beaten till they cried to obedience. The Blacks were not allowed to live the way they wanted. They were not even granted the freedom to travel in their own country, and very often the permission to do so was not granted.

The most poignant aspect of the autobiographies of Daisy Bates and Arthur Corunnas' was the treatment meted out to the Black kids. Children were born, not knowing who fathered them. The women were not only slaves for labour, but also slaves to the White man's desire. The children were more or less orphans as their fathers disowned them and mothers were too busy fighting for survival. If the Black child got into a fight with a White child it was accepted that the Black is wrong. If the child was less than pure Black he was forcibly taken away from his mother and put in a home. This was the government policy as they thought the Aboriginal incapable of hygienic and disciplined parenthood. In the home they were taught never to mention being Aboriginals as it was something to be ashamed of. Very often Aboriginals never saw their children again. Aboriginal girls were sent out as domestic servants once they reached the age of fourteen. Only the White child was thought capable of vocational training. The most heart-rending image is the one conveyed of small Black children crying and begging to be allowed to stay with their mothers, but being harshly pulled away as they clung to their mothers. As domestic servants they were forced to sweep, empty toilets, scrub the floors, scrub the furniture, the pots and pans, clean the hurricane lamps and work in the kitchen. It was a hard life and after all the hard labour, the servants were not given enough to eat. "The people were really hungry sometimes, poor things. They didn't get enough, you see. And they worked hard. You had to work hard. If you didn't do it, then they call the police in to make you work hard. Hunger is a terrible thing." Then Daisy Bates in her story goes on to narrate the cruelty of the Whites: "Nell was a cruel woman, she had a hard heart. When she wasn't whippin' us girls with the bullock cane for not working hard enough, she was hittin' us over the head. She didn't like natives. If one of us was in her way and we didn't move real quick, she'd give us a real hard thump over the head, just like that ooh, it hurt! White people are great ones for thumpin' you on the head, aren't they? We was only kids" (323).

Morgan in her search for identity seeks to expose the injustice and exploitation meted out to the natives by the rulers. Her research provides us in-depth knowledge of the past with its untold stories of the dispossessed and violated. The stories she narrates or re-writes reveal attitudes and living conditions of Aboriginals which are not found in official records or history. As aptly conveyed by Morgan:

> there's almost nothing written from a personal point of view about Aboriginal people. All our history is about the White man. No one knows what it was like for us. A lot of our history has been lost, people have been too frightened to say anything. . . . There are all sorts of files about Aboriginals that go way back, and the government won't release them. . . . And they don't like letting them out, because there are so many instances of police abusing their power when they were supposed to be Protectors of Aborigines that its not funny! I mean, our own government had terrible policies for Aboriginal people. Thousands of families in Australia were destroyed by the government policy of taking children away. None of that happened to White people. (161)

The defining of non-White identity in terms of difference from the White creates a narrative that presents the rage of identities in the process of self-definition. Placing a range of histories, familial and cultural subjectivities usher in an assault on the politics of the centre/dominant. The emphasis and significance of home, loyalty and roots is linked to Morgan's sense of origins and her sense of connection with her own community. Through this sense of belonging, she is speaking for a definable "people." The significance of the concept of 'Place' in the title is one that is central to Morgan's ideas—the longing for, the realization of, a place from which to speak. This place of self and recognition is also a place to claim and to own. It provides the possibility of being an insider. It would be a home for the people who are ostracized as racial outsiders, it is a place to be yourself. This place would provide cultural and racial security. It would be opposed to the histories of exile, longing and displacement. Morgan's intention seems to be to arouse sensitivity to racial discriminations. The themes of native language, self-expression of the natives (Aboriginals) within the community and nation are explored. The role of 'Homes' could be read as colonial institutions, with their imposition of gendered and racial identities, places the text within a wider problematic of First world-Third world politics and power. The book acts as a locus for exploring the difficulties of dialogue between the White imperialists and the Aborigines. Exploitative White policies and realities of racism underlie Morgan's narrative. The conflict between dominant and subordinate races calls for a re-examination of racial discriminations. The layering of antagonisms, of conflicts and struggles that Aboriginals have undergone calls for an awareness of racial inequalities.

Some background information about the Aborigines of Australia would allow a better understanding of the novel. As a result of discoveries, it is believed that the Aborigines must have been in Australia for the last 40,000 years[2]. At the time of White settlement, about 600 dialects were spoken. Aborigine languages do not have words which translate exactly into English words for example the word "own." The connection between the people and land is expressed in terms of "being related to" rather than owning . The subtleness of this conception delayed recognition under Australian law of Aborigine land rights. "Those Aborigines in the desert, they don't want to live like the White man, ownin' this and ownin' that. They just want to live their life free, they don't need the White man's law, they got their own. If they want water in the Gibson Desert, they do a rain song and fill up the places they want." (209) The men were hunters and the meat they caught was shared by the camp, the food gathered by the women was consumed by the smaller immediate family group[3]. Their art comprising of ancestral designs was depicted on bark and sand. (The cover of Morgan's *My Place* represents Aborigine Art). They have a special cultural tradition of rites and customs defined by a special emphasis placed on clanship and their belief in the spiritual significance of the land and its natural features. Specific traditions, rituals, laws and art link the people of each clan to the land they occupy and each clan has various sites of spiritual significance on their land, places to which their spirits return when they die. Australian Aborigines still believe that to destroy or damage a sacred site threatens not only the living but also the spirit inhabitant of the land. Totems are links between Aborigines and their ancestral beings. Each individual has their own totem: fish, snakes, caterpillars, magpies etc. Songs explain how the landscape contains these powerful creator ancestors, who can exert benign or malevolent influence. Totems/ Dreaming, envisaged as reality itself from which life, as we experience it, is derived. The beings that took part in the activities of the Dreaming were referred to as Ancestor Beings. Various oral narratives recording the travels and activities of the Ancestral Beings are passed on from generation to generation. Wisdom and skills obtained over 1000s of years enables the Aborigines to use their environment to the maximum. They had a spiritual affinity with the land and respected the environment . In fact, they were true ecologists. An intimate knowledge of plant harvesting and behaviour of animals ensured that food shortages were rare. They experienced moments of unison with nature. This aspect is further corroborated by Morgan's grandmother sharing a special relationship with the crickets, sound of birds, and the rest of the animal world. She loved the bush and was always curious about the insects, birds, stones the children collected on picnics. They all had a special significance for her.

The division of labour between the men and women amongst the Aborigines gave women the access and right to distribute food and vegetables marking a degree of independence for women and dependence of the men on the produce of women. The community depended on the women to determine camp location, divination and even applied limits to the time men may spend in ritual, all important decisions concerning the lives of the men and the whole group. Another concept of 'Jilmi' or women's housing provided visible proof of women's independence and separateness.[4] This was an area taboo to men, a refuge and home of the ritually important and respected women, which was an expression of women's solidarity. Jilmi life constitutes a complex interplay between woman's need for refuge in a strife-torn community and woman's proud assertions that she is an independent member of her society. It was an assertion of articulate and knowledgeable group of women who were substantially independent of their menfolk in economic and ritual terms. Before White settlement, Aborigine women worked constantly and their contribution made them indispensable to their menfolk. Gradually as an impact of White missionaries, the role of women was classified as one of dependence on men. They became domestic servants to the White master and were sexually exploited.

The Aborigine men had to remove their women from the White man's gaze. So, from a position of independence to vulnerability to protection by their menfolk, the position of women became subordinate. Morgan's grandmother expresses similar sentiments; "We had no protection when we was in service. I know a lot of native servants had kids to White men because they was forced. Makes you want to cry to think how Black women have been treated in this country. It's a terrible thing. They'll pay one day for what they've done." (329).

The plight of women is further exposed in the process of the narration when we are told of the White master Alfred's first wife Eleanor, and his other women Annie and Ginnie, two Aborigine girls who bore him children. Even when it came to work, the boys had it easier, as they were never expected to scrub the floors, nor look after the house, as they were considered to be women's work. A preference for the male child is conveyed at "Bill was overjoyed that he had a son at last" after the birth of two daughters, Sally and Jill. After Bill's death, Billy was "the man of the house" and Morgan says: "We wondered if Billy had special powers we didn't know about." Even Morgan's grandmother shows her preference for the male child. She favoured Billy in the family as did Morgan's father, making Morgan regret being born a girl: "Why was I cursed with being a girl? Nan had a soft spot for Billy, too. It became obvious that what worked for Billy would not work for me."

Morgan's mother was always apprehensive that if she left her husband the children would be taken away from her. She had known what it meant as Aborigine women were not allowed to keep children fathered by a White man. Slavery had a deep-rooted and tremendous impact on the Black families. Slave owners were unconcerned about previous family groupings or other units that existed prior to their conquest. Once the desired destination of enslaving fit men, women and children was reached, the interest of the slave owners was paramount, not any relationship that had previously existed or had been formed between the slaves on their perilous journey. A mother could be wrenched from her child, sibling from sibling. Indeed, it was the habit of slave owners to take slave women for themselves, with no regard either for the slave women or for their own wives, who ironically were safeguarded from the supposed lasciviousness of the Black man. The Blacks were at the mercy of the White owners who rendered them rootless and homeless. This evoked the question of belongingness in Morgan who explores the question of where home is for the generation and how to relate to the home of their ancestors: "I desperately wanted to do something to identify with my new-found heritage and that was the only thing I could think of" when she applied for the Aboriginal scholarship. (134) Despite these crumbs thrown at the Aborigines, the treatment meted out to them is unjust. "Colonialism isn't over yet. We still have a White Australian policy against the Aborigines. They say there is no difference between Black and White, we all Australian. That's a lie. I tell you, the Black man has nothin', the government's been robbin' him blind for years." (209)

There is a relationship between history and literature which when explored gives a clearer picture of any given time than either discipline would have been able to offer independently. *My Place* draws heavily upon the reality of Morgan's existence, of the existence of those around her and reconstructing stories around the past. She focuses on the lives of those who are not in the headlines, but used broad details rooted in lived experience, it dramatizes particular facts of existence, in an effort to expose the ills of racism. Morgan has been raised in ignorance of her ancestry. They spoke English as their mother tongue and have had to write their way back into their language and culture. In her desire to preserve and record the past, she identifies the grandmother as an emblem of the continuing influence of the past. Morgan is concerned about the history of slavery, underdevelopment, exploitation, grief and pain that the Aborigines have undergone.

To conclude, in the words of Edward Hills, "Morgan's prayer for her dying grandmother removes us from all responsibility for the violation of Nan's Aboriginal identity. Because 'Her Place,' her belonging place, is in heaven, the impact of her story lies outside the realm of political and historical consequence." Edward Hills goes on further to answer the question the title of his article poses "What country, friends, is this?" involves a search for narratives that should open up the silences and reverse the denials. If mainstream modes can be exploited by the margins to expose the lives of the forgotten without compromising the integrity of the history, then the past may indeed cease to be another country, mysterious and unexplained."[5]

Thus, we see that Sally Morgan writes about domination and subjugation, of survival in the face of adversity. Her sympathies are with the downtrodden and the victimized. The domination was not only a physical one, but also a subtle, psychological one that was being perpetrated on the Aboriginal people by being regimented, dehumanized and brain-washed by the dominant White ideology. Sally Morgan is concerned about these unpleasant aspects of human life and writes about them., She gives us scenes, taking up slices of day-to-day life for observation and awareness. Deeply committed to the cause of the Aboriginal people, Sally Morgan focuses on how they had a raw deal, how their defences were undermined in various ways and how they had been subjected to physical, psychological and sexual harassment.

NOTES

1. ,Sally Morgan, *My Place* (Western Australia: Fremantle Arts Centre Press, 1987), p. 106.

2. W.H. Edwards, *An Introduction to Aboriginal Societies* (Wentworth Falls: Social Science Press, 1988), p. 1.
3. W.H. Edwards, *An Introduction to Aboriginal Societies* (Wentworth Falls: Social Science Press, 1988), p. 28.
4. Diane Bell, *Daughters of the Dreaming* (St. Leonards: Allen and Unwin, 1993), p. 81.
5. Edward Hills, "What Country, Friends, Is this? Saily Morgan's My Place Revisited," *Journal of Commonwealth Literature*, Volume XXXII, No. 2, 1997, p. 112.